Magic FOR PEOPLE WITH DIABETES
Menus

A. American Diabetes Association.

Publisher	Susan Lau
Editorial Director	Peter Banks
Acquisitions Editor	Susan Reynolds
Co-Editors	Christine B. Welch and Sherrye Landrum
Cover Design	Wickham and Associates
Illustrations	Wickham and Associates
Page Design and Typesetting	Insight Graphics

Reasonable steps have been taken to ensure the accuracy of the information presented; however, the American Diabetes Association cannot ensure the safety or efficacy of any product described in this publication. Individuals are advised to consult a health care professional before undertaking any diet or exercise program. The Association does not endorse any product mentioned by brand name in this book. The American Diabetes Association, its officers, director, employees, contractors, volunteers, and members assume no responsibility or liability for personal or other injury, loss, or damage that may result from the suggestions or information in this publication.

American Diabetes Association
1660 Duke Street
Alexandria, VA 22314

Library of Congress Cataloging-in-Publication Data

Magic menus.
        p.   cm.
Includes index.
ISBN 0-945448-72-4 (pbk.)
1. Diabetes—Diet therapy—Recipes.   I. American Diabetes
Association.
RC662.M333   1996
641.5'6314—dc20
                                            96-42081
                                            CIP

Printed in Canada

1   3   5   7   9   10   8   6   4   2

Table of Contents

Editorial Advisory Board

Peter A. Lodewick, MD
Birmingham, Alabama

Jacqueline Siegel, RN
Seattle, Washington

Samuel L. Abbate, MD, CDE
Marshfield Clinic
Marshfield, Wisconsin

Carolyn Leontos, MS, RD, CDE
Nevada Cooperative Extension
Las Vegas, Nevada

Wylie McNabb, EdD
University of Chicago
Chicago, Illinois

Connie C. Crawley, RD, BS, MS
University of Georgia Extension
Athens, Georgia

John T. Devlin, MD
Maine Medical Center
Portland, Maine

Carol E. Malcom, BSN, CDE
Highline Community Hospital
Seattle, Washington

Lois Jovanovic-Peterson, MD
Sansum Medical Research Foundation
Santa Barbara, California

Virginia Perragallo-Dittko, RN, MA, CDE
Winthrop University Hospital
Mineola, New York

Tim Wysocki, PhD
Nemours Childrens Clinic
Jacksonville, Florida

Acknowledgments

The meals in *Magic Menus* were originally created for the *Month of Meals* series of books by committees of volunteers from the Council on Nutritional Science and Metabolism of the Professional Section of the American Diabetes Association. Committee members, for one or more of the five books, included the following registered dietitians: Marion Franz, MS, RD; Nancy Cooper, RD; Lois Babione, RD; Anne Daly, MS, RD, CDE; Robin Ann Williams, MA, RD, CDE; Marti Chitwood, RD, CDE; Susan L. Thom, RD, KD, CDE; Ruth Kangas, RD, CDE; Carolyn Leontos, MS, RD, CDE; Joyce Cooper, MA, RD; Deborah Fillman, MS, RD, CDE; and Dennis Gordon, RD, CDE.

Most of the recipes were developed by the committee members who worked on *Month of Meals* or were published in *Diabetes Forecast,* the American Diabetes Association's monthly magazine on healthy living with diabetes. The exceptions are noted below.

The recipes for French Dressing, Sloppy Joes, Chicken Cacciatore, Oven-Fried Fish, Crisp Red Cabbage, Meat Loaf, and Gazpacho appear in *American Diabetes Association/American Dietetic Association Family Cookbook, Volume I,* © 1980 by the American Diabetes Association, Inc., and The American Dietetic Association, Inc., and are used with permission of the publisher, Prentice Hall Press.

The recipes for Crunchy Granola, Cheesy Grits, Apple-Raisin Muffins, Fluffy High-Fiber Pancakes, Noodle Supreme Salad, Black Bean Soup, Chicken Tacos, Oven-Fried Chicken, Vegetarian Lasagna, and Herbed Pork Kabobs appear in *American Diabetes Association/American Dietetic Association Family Cookbook, Volume II,* © 1984 by the American Diabetes Association, Inc., and The American Dietetic Association, Inc., and are used with permission of the publisher, Prentice Hall Press.

The recipes for Scones, Minestrone, Pears Filled With Strawberry Cream Cheese, Nutty Rice Loaf, Crab Cakes, Spinach-Stuffed Chicken Breasts, and New England Chicken Croquettes appear in *American Diabetes Association/American Dietetic Association Family Cookbook, Volume III*, © 1987 by the American Diabetes Association, Inc., and The American Dietetic Association, Inc., and are used with permission of the publisher, Prentice Hall Press.

The recipes for Whole-Wheat Pizza and Noodle Pudding appear in *American Diabetes Association Holiday Cookbook*, by Betty Wedman, MS, RD, © 1986 by the American Diabetes Association, Inc.

The recipes for Chocolate Angel Food Cake and Spicy Black-Eyed Peas were published in *Southern Living* magazine and are used with permission of *Southern Living* magazine.

The recipe for Tofu Garden Quiche appears in *More Calculated Cooking*, by Jeanne Jones, © 1981 by Jeanne Jones, and is used with permission of the publisher, 101 Productions/Cole Group, Inc., Santa Rosa, California.

The following recipes are used with permission of their creators: Fiesta Rice, Chicken Ratatouille, and Mike's Veal by Mike Connor; Light and Creamy Yogurt Pie and Saucy Seafood Stir-Fry by Kathy England; Squash Casserole by Cathy Marett; Frosty Grapes by Cindy McAllister; Vegetable Stir-Fry by Shawn McLemore; Chocolate-Flavored Syrup by Debbie Pierce; Black Bean Dip by Judy Sharpe; Schinkennudelin by Dominica Uhlig; and Stuffed Zucchini by Jeff Spoon.

For information on ordering *Magic Menus* or any of the *Month of Meals* books, call 1-800-232-6733. For information on joining the American Diabetes Association (ADA), call 1-800-806-7801.

People with diabetes can eat almost anything—including packaged foods, such as frozen entrees—as long as their overall diet is well balanced. As a convenient aid to readers who want fast yet healthy meal choices, *Magic Menus* includes some brand names or product names. The use of selected brand names does not mean that they are the only brands suitable for people with diabetes. Although we tried to be sure that these packaged foods met the calorie levels of individual menus, ADA does not endorse these products or guarantee that they are appropriate for all people with diabetes. You are encouraged to read food labels carefully and to consult with a registered dietitian to determine whether a food fits into your meal plans.

Introduction

Most cookbooks give you lots of recipes and only a few suggestions for combining them into a day's meals. When you find a recipe you like, you still must choose other foods to round out the meal. People with diabetes have the added challenge of counting the carbohydrate in the meal so they'll know what effect it will have on their blood glucose level. A simple but unexciting solution is to eat the same things day after day. A better solution is found in this book and the other books in this series. The menus are counted and balanced for you. Just cook and eat.

Magic Menus will help you choose healthy foods to make up your daily menus easily. You will find many menus that can be prepared quickly, menus built around favorite family dishes, meatless menus, and menus emphasizing low-fat and high-fiber foods. For people who cook for just one or two, most of these recipes can be prepared and then divided into serving sizes and frozen for quick, no-fuss future meals.

There are complete menus for breakfast, lunch, dinner, and snacks. One day's menu selections—breakfast, lunch, dinner, and a snack—provides approximately 1,500 calories. Directions are given for adjusting the menus to other calorie levels. Each day's menus will provide about 45–50 percent of your calories from carbohydrate, 20 percent from protein, and about 30 percent from fat. They follow the 1994 American Diabetes Association Nutritional Recommendations for People With Diabetes and the 1990 Dietary Guidelines for Americans (U.S. Dept. of Agriculture and U.S. Dept. of Health and Human Services, Home and Garden Bulletin 232).

These menus will help you

■ **Eat a variety of foods.** Eating a wide variety of different foods helps you get all the essential vitamins, minerals, and nutrients your body needs. Variety also helps keep your interest so that your diet doesn't become boring. With *Magic Menus,* you can mix and match thousands of combinations of breakfasts, lunches, and dinners.

■ **Maintain a healthy weight.** *Magic Menus* allows you to add and subtract snacks to get just the right number of calories for you to achieve and maintain a healthy body weight.

■ **Choose a diet low in fat, saturated fat, and cholesterol.** The meals in *Magic Menus* average less than 300 milligrams of cholesterol per day and less than 30 percent total fat. These menus emphasize choosing low-fat foods.

■ **Choose a diet with plenty of vegetables, fruits, and whole-grain products.** These foods not only add variety to your diet, but they can be an important source of fiber. Unrefined foods are close in form to what Mother Nature gives us, and the closer to the source, the better.

■ **Use sugars only in moderation.** It's okay to eat sugar as part of a balanced meal. But you still need to watch empty calories and the amount of carbohydrate you eat. That's why most of these recipes are low in sugar. Simple desserts containing limited amounts of sugar are included. Instead of sugar, you can also use artificial sweeteners that have essentially no calories, such as aspartame (Equal or NutraSweet), acesulfame-K (Sweet One or Sunette), and saccharin (Sweet 'n Low, Sugar Twin, or Sweet 10).

■ **Use salt and sodium only in moderation.** Most of the menus call for a moderate amount of salt. Menus containing higher-than-recommended sodium levels are for occasional use. Eating three healthy meals a day will provide all the sodium you need without using the salt shaker. Gradually cut back on the salt you add at the table and in your cooking so your taste buds have time to adjust to a lower level of sodium.

The Six Food Groups

The menus in *Magic Menus* have been developed using a meal-planning system that divides foods into six groups: Starch, Meat and Meat Substitutes, Vegetables, Fruit, Milk, and Fat. Foods are placed into one group or another based on their nutrient makeup—carbohydrate, protein, fat, and calories.

Starch. This group includes whole grains (brown rice, bulgur wheat, wheat berries, oats, barley), cereal, pasta, rice, breads, starchy vegetables (potatoes, corn, lima beans, and winter squashes such as acorn and spaghetti), crackers, desserts, and many snack-type foods.

Meat and Meat Substitutes. This group includes beef, pork, lamb, veal, poultry, fish, seafood, eggs, tofu, cheese, cottage cheese, and peanut butter. Foods are then divided into lean, medium-fat, and high-fat choices.

Vegetables. The vegetable group is made up of nonstarchy vegetables, either raw or cooked, such as broccoli, asparagus, green beans, cabbage, carrots, salad greens, onions, tomatoes, and summer squashes like crookneck and zucchini.

Fruit. This group includes all varieties of fruit—fresh, frozen, canned, and dried—as well as fruit juices.

Milk. Included here are milk, yogurt, and buttermilk.

Fat. You have obvious fats like margarine, butter, cooking oils, mayonnaise, and salad dressings plus other high-fat foods like avocados, olives, nuts and seeds, bacon, sour cream, and cream cheese.

For a complete listing of foods and serving sizes in the six food groups, see *Exchange Lists for Meal Planning*, available from the American Diabetes Association or The American

Dietetic Association, or contact a registered dietitian. If you plan to adjust the meals in this book (see pages 8–11), you'll need to know what nutrients are in a serving from each of the food groups. This information is found in *Exchange Lists for Meal Planning*.

Food Group	Calories	Per Serving Carbo-hydrate (grams)	Protein (grams)	Fat (grams)
Starch	80	15	3	trace
Meat and Substitutes				
Lean	55		7	3
Medium Fat	75		7	5
High Fat	100			
Vegetables	25	5	2	
Fruit	60	15		
Milk				
Skim	90	12	8	trace
Low Fat (1%)	102	12	8	3
Whole	150	12	8	8
Fat	45			5

Guidelines for Good Nutrition

Good nutrition comes from eating a variety of foods. No single food will supply all of the nutrients your body needs; therefore, you should eat from each of the food groups every day. It's also a good idea to vary the foods you eat within each food group from day to day. For example, eat an apple or orange from time to time instead of always having a banana. Here are some more guidelines to healthy food choices.

Eat less fat. You'll note that this book presents low-fat meals and recommends that you use products such as reduced-calorie salad dressings. The menus also average less than 300 milligrams of cholesterol a day. This assumes you limit your eggs to three or fewer a week, not counting the eggs you use in cooking.

To cut back on fat, you can
- Eat smaller portions of meat.
- Eat fish and poultry (without the skin) more often.
- Choose lean cuts of red meat.
- Prepare meats by broiling, roasting, or baking instead of frying. Trim off all fat before cooking and remove the skin from poultry before eating it.
- Avoid adding fat in cooking.
- Avoid fried foods.
- Avoid sauces or gravy.
- Eat fewer high-fat foods, such as cold cuts, bacon, sausage, hot dogs, butter, mayonnaise, nuts, salad dressing, lard, and solid shortening.
- Drink skim or 1% milk.
- Eat less ice cream, cheese, sour cream, cream, whole milk, and other high-fat dairy products. Use low- or nonfat yogurt or low-fat cottage cheese instead of sour cream. Use low-fat cheeses.

- Use 1 tablespoon of regular salad dressing or 2 tablespoons of reduced-calorie salad dressing. You can have more of salad dressings that contain less than 6 calories per tablespoon.
- Use butter-flavored granules (Butter Buds or Molly McButter) to season vegetables, potatoes, rice, or noodles.
- Use ¼ cup egg substitute in place of each egg in a recipe.

Eat more high-fiber foods. *Magic Menus* includes lots of high-fiber foods—fruits, vegetables, and whole-grain products—in the meals. In general,
- Eat more whole-grain breads, cereals, and crackers. Eat more dried beans, peas, and lentils, too.
- Eat high-fiber foods, such as oat bran, brown rice, wild rice, barley, and bulgur.
- Eat more vegetables (raw and cooked). You can have large servings of raw, nonstarchy vegetables when called for in a menu, which may include salad greens, carrot or celery sticks, tomatoes, cucumbers, green peppers, radishes, and the like.
- Eat whole fruit instead of drinking fruit juice.

Eat less sugar. Because you want the foods you eat to give you nutrients as well as calories, this book provides recipes that are low in sugar. The menus also use sugar-free or no-sugar-added syrups and jellies and fresh and/or unsweetened fruits. In general,
- Choose fresh fruit or fruit canned in juice or water.
- Limit no-sugar-added fruit spreads (jams or jellies) to 1–2 teaspoons of those that are 20 calories or less per serving.
- Use less table sugar, honey, syrup, jam, jelly, candy, sweet rolls, fruit canned in syrup, regular gelatin desserts, cake with icing, pie, and other high-calorie sweets.
- Avoid regular soft drinks (one 12-ounce can has 9 teaspoons of sugar). To these meals, you can add your choice of calorie-free beverages, such as coffee, hot or iced tea, mineral water, diet sodas, and sugar-free flavored seltzers.
- Try sweeteners that don't have any calories.

Use less salt. Using the menus in this book, your total daily intake of sodium will be between 2,000 and 3,000 milligrams. In general,

■ Try not to put salt on food at the table.

■ Use less salt when cooking. Season recipes with your favorite spices instead. Try basil, dill, lemon pepper, paprika, fresh herbs, and fresh garlic or garlic powder. Be sure to choose low-salt varieties when herb mixtures are purchased.

■ Eat fewer high-salt foods, such as canned soups, ham, sauerkraut, hot dogs, pickles, and foods that taste salty. Choose reduced-fat and reduced-sodium varieties of these foods.

■ Eat fewer convenience and fast foods.

The recipes in this book use these standard abbreviations:

Tbsp = tablespoon
tsp = teaspoon
oz = ounce
lb = pound
qt = quart

How to Use This Book

Magic Menus allows you to choose the calorie level that best meets your needs. First, you need to know how many calories you require daily. The best way to do this is to meet with a registered dietitian or certified diabetes educator, who can design a meal plan with the right number of calories for your nutritional needs.

BASIC MEAL PLAN: 1,500 CALORIES A DAY
Each breakfast, lunch, and dinner in *Magic Menus* has about the same number of calories as the other breakfasts, or lunches, or dinners, so you can mix and match them to suit your own tastes. One day's breakfast, lunch, and dinner add up to about 1,350 calories. By adding two 60-calorie snacks OR one 125-calorie snack, your daily total will be 1,500 calories—the Basic Meal Plan. Choose any menus you like. All the portions on the menus are for one person, so you can have everything listed.

If you need more or fewer calories than the basic 1,500-calorie menus provide, no problem. Adjusting meals to meet your requirements is as easy as following the instructions on the next few pages.

Basic Meal Plan Plus
If you are following a meal plan that allows you 1,800 calories a day, use the chart below to adjust the Basic Meal Plan.

First, choose any menu in *Magic Menus* that you want. Then, move down the 1,800-calorie column and follow the directions. Breakfast, lunch, and dinner are the same as in the Basic Meal Plan. The extra calories you need will come from snacks—a 125-calorie morning snack, a 125-calorie afternoon snack, and a 170-calorie evening snack.

The chart also shows you how to reach a 2,100-calorie meal plan. You may want to alter this plan to meet your needs if you are pregnant or breastfeeding.

Meal	1,500 Calories (Basic Meal Plan)	1,800 Calories	2,100 Calories
Breakfast	Total calories: 350	Same as Basic Meal Plan Total calories: 350	Add 1 Starch OR 1 Meat to the Basic Meal Plan Total calories: 450
Morning Snack		Add 1 125-calorie snack Total calories: 125	Add 1 60-calorie snack Total calories: 60
Lunch	Total calories: 450	Same as Basic Meal Plan Total calories: 450	Add 1 Starch AND 1 Fat to the Basic Meal Plan Total calories: 575
Afternoon Snack		Add 1 125-calorie snack Total calories: 125	Add 1 125-calorie snack Total calories: 125
Dinner	Total calories: 550	Same as Basic Meal Plan Total calories: 550	Add 1 Starch AND 1 Milk to the Basic Meal Plan Total calories: 720
Evening Snack	2 60-calorie snacks OR 1 125-calorie snack Total calories: 125	Add 1 170-calorie snack Total calories: 170	Add 1 170-calorie snack Total calories: 170

Basic Meal Plan Minus

If you are following a meal plan of 1,200 calories a day, use the chart on the next page to adjust the Basic Meal Plan. To meet your body's nutrient needs, you need to eat at least 1,200 calories a day.

First, choose any menu in *Magic Menus* that you want. Then, move down the 1,200-calorie column and follow the directions: Take away 1 Starch or 1 Milk from breakfast in the Basic Meal Plan. Take away 1 Fruit at lunch from the Basic Meal Plan. Take away 1 Fat at dinner from the Basic Meal Plan. There are no snacks in the 1,200-calorie meal plan. If small snacks help you control your blood glucose better, ask your dietitian if you can save an item from a meal to eat at snack time. That way your daily calories don't change, but you have spread the food out over the day. This may keep you from feeling hungry, too.

This chart also shows you how to reach a 1,350-calorie meal plan.

Meal	1,200 Calories	1,350 Calories	1,500 Calories (Basic Meal Plan)
Breakfast	Take away 1 Starch OR 1 Milk from Basic Meal Plan Total calories: 270	Same as Basic Meal Plan Total calories: 350	Total calories: 350
Morning Snack			
Lunch	Take away 1 Fruit from Basic Meal Plan Total calories: 390	Same as Basic Meal Plan Total calories: 450	Total calories: 450
Afternoon Snack			
Dinner	Take away 1 Fat from Basic Meal Plan Total calories: 505	Same as Basic Meal Plan Total calories: 550	Total calories: 550
Evening Snack			2 60-calorie snacks OR 1 125-calorie snack Total calories: 125

Sample Meal Plan 1

Here's how to adjust the Basic Meal Plan (1,500 calories) for about 1,200 calories.

Meal	**Calories**

Breakfast
(Plus or minus)   350
-1____ Starch____ serving(s)
(type of serving)   -80   Subtotal ___270___

Lunch
(Plus or minus)   450
-1____ Fruit____ serving(s)
(type of serving)   -60   Subtotal ___390___

Dinner
(Plus or minus)   550
-1____ Fat_____ serving(s)
(type of serving)   -45   Subtotal ___505___

Total Daily Calories ___1,165___

Sample Meal Plan 2

Here's how to adjust the Basic Meal Plan (1,500 calories) for about 2,200 calories.

Meal	**Calories**	

Breakfast
(Plus or minus)   350
<u>+1</u>   <u>Starch</u>   serving(s)
(type of serving)   +80   Subtotal   430

Lunch
(Plus or minus)   450
<u>+1</u>   <u>Fat</u>   serving(s)
(type of serving)   +60

<u>+1</u>   <u>Fruit</u>   serving(s)
(type of serving)   +45   Subtotal   555

Dinner
(Plus or minus)   550
<u>+1</u>   <u>Starch</u>   serving(s)
(type of serving)   +80

<u>+1</u>   <u>Meat</u>   serving(s)
(type of serving)   +75

<u>+1</u>   <u>Fat</u>   serving(s)
(type of serving)   +45   Subtotal   750

Snacks (Morning, Afternoon, and/or Evening)
(Plus or minus)   125
<u>+2</u>   <u>Starch</u>   serving(s)
(type of serving)

<u>+2</u>   <u>Milk or Meat</u>   serving(s)
(type of serving)   340   Subtotal   465

Total Daily Calories   2,200

Your Meal Plan

Meal	Calories

Meal   **Calories**

Breakfast
(Plus or minus)

_____ _____ serving(s)   _____
(type of serving)   _____   Subtotal _____

Morning Snack
(Plus or minus)

_____ _____ serving(s)   _____
(type of serving)   _____   Subtotal _____

Lunch
(Plus or minus)

_____ _____ serving(s)   _____
(type of serving)   _____

_____ _____ serving(s)
(type of serving)   _____   Subtotal _____

Afternoon Snack
(Plus or minus)

_____ _____ serving(s)   _____
(type of serving)   _____

_____ _____ serving(s)
(type of serving)   _____   Subtotal _____

Dinner
(Plus or minus)

_____ _____ serving(s)   _____
(type of serving)   _____

_____ _____ serving(s)
(type of serving)   _____

_____ _____ serving(s)
(type of serving)   _____   Subtotal _____

Evening Snack
(Plus or minus)

_____ _____ serving(s)   _____
(type of serving)   _____   Subtotal _____

Total Daily Calories _____

*B*reakfast

Each breakfast in this section has about 350 calories and includes
2 Starch servings
1 Fruit serving
1 Skim Milk serving
1 Fat serving

Total Fat: 5 grams

Total Carbohydrate: 57 grams

Protein: 14 grams

Some menus have 1 Meat serving instead of 1 Skim Milk or 1 Starch serving.

No-Fuss Mornings

¾ cup cornflakes with
1 cup skim or 1% milk
1 slice whole-wheat toast with
1 tsp margarine
1 cup cantaloupe cubes

4½-inch-square waffle
1¼ cups fresh strawberries
½ cup plain nonfat yogurt
3 Tbsp Grape-Nuts cereal
½ cup skim or 1% milk

Top waffle with mixture of strawberries and yogurt. Sprinkle with Grape-Nuts.

1 slice whole-wheat toast with
1 tsp no-sugar-added fruit spread and
1 Tbsp reduced-calorie margarine
1 egg or ¼ cup egg substitute, scrambled
    with
Nonstick vegetable spray
½ grapefruit
1 cup skim or 1% milk

4

1 cup cooked oatmeal with
Dash cinnamon and brown sugar substitute
   (optional)
1 Tbsp raisins
¼ cup applesauce
1 cup skim or 1% milk

5

2 slices French toast with
1 Tbsp reduced-calorie margarine or 1 tsp
   margarine and
2 Tbsp sugar-free syrup (optional)
½ cup no-sugar-added applesauce with
Dash cinnamon
1 cup skim or 1% milk

*Dip 2 slices of bread in beaten egg. Brown on both sides in a
pan coated with nonstick vegetable cooking spray.*

6

1 slice whole-wheat toast with
2 tsp no-sugar-added fruit spread and
1 tsp margarine
1 cup nonfat artificially sweetened fruit-
   flavored yogurt topped with
3 Tbsp wheat germ and
½ sliced banana

4 4-inch pancakes with
¾ cup blueberries, fresh or frozen,
   unsweetened
1 cup skim or 1% milk

To make a blueberry sauce, microwave blueberries briefly, until they thicken to desired consistency.

1 English muffin with
1 tsp no-sugar-added fruit spread and
1 tsp margarine
1 serving Strawberry Blender Drink

Combine 1 cup skim or 1% milk and 1¼ cups strawberries, fresh or frozen, no sugar added, in a blender and blend until smooth and creamy.

1 poached egg
1 whole-wheat English muffin with
1 tsp margarine
1 fresh pear

1½ cups puffed rice with
1 cup skim or 1% milk
½ English muffin with
½ Tbsp peanut butter
1 medium nectarine

½ cup cooked grits
1 slice whole-wheat toast with
1 tsp margarine
1 oz cheddar cheese
½ cup orange juice

Breakfast Tortilla:
    ½ cup egg substitute, scrambled with
    2 Tbsp chopped onion and
    2 Tbsp chopped green pepper and
    2 Tbsp salsa, wrapped in
    2 6-inch soft tortillas
1 kiwifruit

1 cup cooked kasha, oat groats, brown rice,
  or wheat berries with
2 Tbsp raisins and
2 Tbsp walnuts, chopped
Dash cinnamon and artificial sweetener
  (optional)
1 cup skim or 1% milk

Whole grains require 30–45 minutes of cooking. To speed up breakfast, cook cereal the night before, then heat up in the morning. Other alternatives are to pour hot water over grains the night before to soften them and save time the next morning or to cook them overnight in a slow cooker or Crock-Pot.

1 2-oz pumpernickel bagel with
1½ Tbsp low-fat cream cheese
3 medium stewed prunes
1 cup skim or 1% milk

Old-Fashioned Strawberry Shortcake:
1 3-inch biscuit
1¼ cups sliced strawberries
1 cup skim or 1% milk
Artificial sweetener as desired

Split biscuit and place half in a bowl. Cover with half of strawberries, then top with other half of biscuit. Cover with remaining strawberries and pour milk over biscuit and strawberries.

3 Tbsp Grape-Nuts cereal in
1 cup low-fat artificially sweetened lemon
    yogurt with
¾ cup water-packed mandarin oranges
1 piece whole-wheat toast with
1 tsp margarine

Cinnamon Tortilla Pocket:
  1 6-inch tortilla filled with
  ¼ cup ricotta cheese blended with
  ½ pkg. artificial sweetener and
  ¼ tsp cinnamon
¾ cup fresh pineapple, mango, kiwifruit,
  banana, and/or papaya

Spread mixture down middle of tortilla; fold four corners over into a square and microwave on low for 30 seconds until warm.

2 Cheese Cornucopias:
  2 slices bread
  1 oz low-fat cheese, grated
  2 toothpicks
  1 tsp soft margarine
½ cup orange juice

Trim crusts from bread and sprinkle with cheese. Fold bread to opposite corners and secure with a toothpick. Spread top with margarine. Place on tray in toaster oven at 350 degrees until brown, about 10 minutes. Remove toothpicks to serve.

Bacon and Egg Sandwich:
  2 slices high-fiber bread, toasted
  1 egg, cooked in nonstick pan
  1 strip bacon, cooked crisp
1 medium tangelo

Breakfast Parfait:
  8 oz nonfat artificially sweetened vanilla
    yogurt
  4 pecan halves, chopped
  ½ banana, sliced
  3 Tbsp wheat germ
3 graham crackers (2½-inch squares)

Layer yogurt, pecans, banana, and wheat germ in a parfait glass.

Commuter Breakfast:
  1 Tbsp peanut butter
  1 cup nonfat plain yogurt
  ½ banana (or ½ cup other fruit)
  3 or 4 ice cubes (optional)
  Artificial sweetener, if desired
  ⅓ cup All-Bran cereal

Blend all ingredients except cereal in a blender. Pour in mug, then top with cereal.

2 cups puffed kasha
¾ cup blueberries
1 cup skim or 1% milk

2 frozen waffles topped with
½ cup no-sugar-added applesauce
1 oz Canadian bacon

½ cup cooked oatmeal with
3 Tbsp wheat germ,
6 almonds, chopped,
½ banana, sliced, and
Cinnamon to taste
1 cup skim or 1% milk

1 Sugarless Blueberry Muffin
½ cup bran flakes with
1 cup skim or 1% milk
½ cup fresh pineapple chunks

Sugarless Blueberry Muffins

Yield: 12 muffins / Serving size: 1 muffin

INGREDIENTS

Nonstick vegetable cooking spray
1 cup blueberries, picked over and rinsed
1¾ cups plus 2 tsp all-purpose flour
1 Tbsp baking powder
¼ tsp nutmeg
¼ tsp cinnamon
2 eggs
¼ cup vegetable oil
¾ cup orange juice
1 tsp grated lemon or orange rind

METHOD

1. Preheat oven to 400 degrees. Spray muffin tin with vegetable spray or line with baking cups.
2. Lightly coat the blueberries with 2 tsp flour by shaking together in a paper bag.
3. In a large bowl, stir together 1¾ cups flour, baking powder, nutmeg, and cinnamon.
4. In a small bowl, beat the eggs lightly. Add oil, orange juice, and grated rind.
5. Add the liquid to the dry mixture and stir gently. Before the two mixtures are fully combined, fold in the blueberries.
6. Fill each muffin cup about two-thirds full. Bake 20–25 minutes.

1 cinnamon-raisin bagel with
¼ cup **Ricotta Cheese Spread**
½ cup orange juice

Ricotta Cheese Spread

Yield: ¼ cup / Serving size: ¼ cup

INGREDIENTS

¼ cup part-skim ricotta cheese
1 pkg. artificial sweetener
⅛ tsp vanilla (or other flavoring)
Dash cinnamon

METHOD

1. Mix first three ingredients together.
2. Spread on bagel halves. Sprinkle with cinnamon.
3. Heat under broiler until hot, about 1–2 minutes.

1 serving **Easy Spud Breakfast**
1 slice whole-grain toast
1 tsp reduced-calorie margarine
¾ cup mixed berries

Easy Spud Breakfast

Yield: 2 servings / Serving size: ½ recipe

INGREDIENTS

1 large baked potato with skin
Nonstick vegetable cooking spray
¼ cup chopped onions
¼ cup chopped green or red peppers
1 oz lean ham, chopped
1 egg
2 Tbsp grated reduced-fat cheddar cheese
Fresh or dried parsley

METHOD

1. Slice baked potato in half the long way. Scoop out one-third of the potato pulp (save for another meal). Set shells on a microwave-safe dish.
2. Spray a nonstick skillet with vegetable spray and sauté onions and peppers for about 5 minutes or until soft.
3. Add ham and sauté another 1–2 minutes. Add the beaten egg and cook until egg is done. Add salt and pepper to taste.
4. Fill each potato half with egg mixture. Top with grated cheese. Heat at 400 degrees in a conventional oven, or microwave until hot. Garnish with parsley.

2 **Scones** with
½ cup pineapple juice
1 Tbsp reduced-calorie margarine
1 cup skim or 1% milk

Scones

Yield: 16 scones / Serving size: 1 scone

INGREDIENTS
3 Tbsp margarine
2 cups all-purpose flour
1½ tsp baking powder
½ tsp baking soda
1 pkg. artificial sweetener
¼–½ tsp salt
½ cup skim or 1% milk
¼ cup dark raisins or currants
¼ tsp orange peel
Nonstick vegetable spray

METHOD
1. Preheat oven to 450 degrees.
2. In food processor or with pastry blender, mix margarine and flour until the mixture resembles coarse crumbs. Stir in baking powder, baking soda, and artificial sweetener, and salt to taste.
3. Stir in milk until dry ingredients are moistened. Stir in raisins and orange peel.
4. Gather dough into a ball. Roll out on a lightly floured board to ½ inch thickness. Cut into rounds using a 2½-inch cookie cutter. Place on cookie sheet well coated with vegetable spray.
5. Bake 7–10 minutes or until lightly browned.

2 Graham Pudding Sandwiches
½ cup apple juice
½ cup skim or 1% milk

Graham Pudding Sandwiches

Yield: 32 sandwiches / Serving size: 1 sandwich

INGREDIENTS

1 pkg. sugar-free instant pudding, prepared
½ cup no-sugar-added peanut butter
64 graham cracker squares

METHOD

1. Prepare pudding according to package directions. Mix in ½ cup peanut butter.
2. Spread 1 Tbsp mixture on 1 graham cracker square and top with another graham cracker square. Freeze. Eat frozen or slightly thawed.

1 small plain muffin with
2 tsp no-sugar-added fruit spread
1 cup **Breakfast Blender Drink**

Breakfast Blender Drink

Yield: 1 serving / Serving size: 1 cup

INGREDIENTS

1 cup skim or 1% milk
½ banana, frozen and sliced
3 Tbsp wheat germ
½ tsp vanilla

METHOD

1. Combine all ingredients in blender and blend until
   smooth and creamy.

31

⅓ cup **Crunchy Granola**
¾ cup vegetable juice
1 cup skim or 1% milk

Crunchy Granola

Yield: 16 servings / Serving size: ⅓ cup

INGREDIENTS

3½ cups rolled oats
½ cup wheat germ
½ cup coconut
¼ cup sesame seeds
¼ cup almonds
¼ cup sunflower or millet seeds
¼ cup honey
¼ cup oil
1 Tbsp vanilla
½ cup raisins

METHOD

1. Mix all ingredients except raisins together with electric mixer. Spread evenly on 2 baking sheets with edges. Bake in 250-degree oven until golden brown (45–60 minutes).
2. Turn and stir after 30 minutes.
3. Remove from oven and add raisins. Cool and store in plastic bag.

1 cup **Cheesy Grits**
½ grapefruit

Cheesy Grits

Yield: 2 servings / Serving size: 1 cup

INGREDIENTS

2 cups water
½ cup quick grits
¾ cup shredded cheddar cheese
1 Tbsp margarine
2 Tbsp chopped green chilies or picante sauce
1 egg, separated
¼ cup skim or 1% milk

METHOD

1. Bring water to boil in heavy saucepan. Stir in grits.
   Return to a boil. Reduce heat, partially cover, and cook
   5 minutes. Stir occasionally.
2. Add cheese, margarine, and chilies. Stir until cheese is
   melted.
3. Beat egg yolk with milk and stir into grits.
4. Whip egg white until stiff and fold into mixture.
5. Pour into lightly greased 5- by 5-inch casserole dish and
   bake in 350-degree oven for 1 hour. Let set 5 minutes
   before cutting.

Note: Due to high fat content, limit this dish to occasional
use. To reduce fat, use half servings.

1 Apple-Raisin Muffin
½ cup bran flakes with
1 cup skim or 1% milk

Apple-Raisin Muffins

Yield: 12 muffins / Serving size: 1 muffin

INGREDIENTS

Nonstick vegetable cooking spray
2 cups all-purpose flour
1 Tbsp baking powder
¼ tsp salt
1 tsp cinnamon
3 pkgs. artificial sweetener
1 egg
3 Tbsp corn oil
½ cup skim or 1% milk
1 cup no-sugar-added applesauce
½ cup raisins, washed and drained

METHOD

1. Preheat oven to 400 degrees. Prepare 2½-inch muffin tins by spraying with vegetable spray.
2. Combine dry ingredients in mixing bowl and mix thoroughly.
3. Beat egg and whip in oil, milk, and applesauce.
4. Add liquid mixture to dry ingredients and mix until flour is moistened. Stir in raisins.
5. Fill muffin tins two-thirds full. Bake for 25 minutes. Remove muffins from tin immediately. Store muffins in freezer for later use.

1 serving **Creamed Chipped Beef Over Toast**

¾ cup equal parts berries and cubed melon

Creamed Chipped Beef Over Toast

Yield: 2 servings / Serving size: ½ recipe

INGREDIENTS

2 oz dried beef
2 tsp butter or margarine
1 Tbsp flour
1 cup skim or 1% milk
2 slices whole-wheat toast

METHOD

1. Pour enough hot water over beef to cover. Soak for 20–30 minutes. Pour off water and slice beef into strips.
2. Melt butter in a small saucepan. Stir in flour with a wooden spoon until well mixed.
3. Add milk a little at a time until all milk is added.
4. Add beef and heat until bubbly.
5. Cut toast in half and pour beef over toast.

2 Angel Biscuits
½ broiled grapefruit
1 cup skim or 1% milk

Angel Biscuits

Yield: 36 biscuits / Serving size: 1 biscuit

INGREDIENTS
1 pkg. yeast
2 Tbsp warm water
5 cups all-purpose whole-wheat flour
1 tsp baking soda
3 tsp baking powder
4 Tbsp sugar
1 tsp salt
1 cup shortening
2 cups buttermilk
Melted butter to brush tops (optional)

METHOD
1. Preheat oven to 400 degrees.
2. Dissolve yeast in lukewarm water.
3. Sift flour, soda, baking powder, sugar, and salt into bowl. Cut in shortening.
4. Add buttermilk, then yeast mixture. Stir until all flour is dampened.
5. Knead on floured board for 1–2 minutes. Roll out to desired thickness and cut with biscuit cutter, or refrigerate dough in an airtight container and use as needed (dough will keep several days).
6. If desired, brush with melted butter before or after baking. Bake about 12–15 minutes.

1 serving **Spanish Omelette**
2 slices rye toast with
1 tsp margarine
½ cup orange sections

Spanish Omelette

Yield: 4 servings / Serving size: ¼ recipe

INGREDIENTS

½ cup chopped green pepper
¼ cup chopped onion
1 Tbsp garlic, minced
2 Tbsp water
1 can green chilies, chopped
½ small tomato, squeezed of juice and chopped
2 tsp chopped pimento
6 egg whites
Pinch of saffron
½ cup low-fat cottage cheese

METHOD

1. In nonstick skillet, sauté green pepper, onion, and garlic in water. Add chilies, tomato, and pimento and boil off remaining liquid.
2. Combine egg whites and saffron and beat into soft peaks. Fold cottage cheese into egg whites, followed by the contents of the skillet.
3. Return to skillet and fry until eggs are set, turning to avoid scorching. Pour off any water rendered during cooking and serve.

2 frozen pancakes with
2 Tbsp reduced-calorie syrup
1 serving **Grapefruit Grand**
1 cup skim or 1% milk

Grapefruit Grand

Yield: 1 serving

INGREDIENTS
½ grapefruit
1 tsp artificial sweetener
Dash cinnamon

METHOD
1. Top grapefruit with artificial sweetener and cinnamon.
   Broil grapefruit for about 2 minutes.

1 serving **Broccoli Quiche**
½ English muffin with
1 tsp margarine
1 cup mixed melons and berries

Broccoli Quiche

Yield: 6 servings / Serving size: ⅙ recipe

INGREDIENTS

1 10-oz pkg. frozen cut broccoli
Nonstick vegetable cooking spray
½ cup chopped green pepper
⅓ cup chopped onion
1 cup shredded Colby cheese
1 cup skim or 1% milk
½ cup biscuit mix
3 eggs or ¾ cup egg substitute
¼ tsp salt
¼ tsp pepper

METHOD

1. Cook broccoli according to package directions; drain.
2. Place broccoli in 9-inch pie plate coated with vegetable spray; sprinkle with green pepper, onion, and cheese. Set aside.
3. Combine remaining ingredients in an electric blender; blend 15 seconds or until smooth. Pour over broccoli mixture.
4. Bake at 375 degrees for 25–30 minutes or until set. Let stand 5 minutes before serving.

2 4-inch **Fluffy High-Fiber, Low-Fat Pancakes** with
½ cup strawberry topping and
1 tsp margarine
1 cup skim or 1% milk

Fluffy High-Fiber, Low-Fat Pancakes

Yield: 8 4-inch pancakes / Serving size: 2 pancakes

INGREDIENTS

1 cup buttermilk or sour skim or 1% milk (add 1 Tbsp lemon juice per 1 cup milk)

½ cup quick-cooking rolled oats

⅔ cup miller's bran (unprocessed, uncooked wheat bran)

1 egg

¼ cup whole-wheat flour

½ tsp sugar

¼ tsp salt

¾ tsp baking soda

1 cup strawberries, fresh or frozen, no sugar added

1 tsp apple juice concentrate

METHOD

1. Combine buttermilk, oats, and bran in large mixing bowl. Let stand 5 minutes. Add egg and beat until blended.
2. Mix flour, sugar, salt, and baking soda until blended.
3. Add to bran mixture and blend until flour is moistened.
4. Pour ¼ cup batter on lightly greased, preheated 375-degree frying pan. Cook about 3 minutes or until bubbles form and edge of pancake is dry. Turn and cook 2 minutes longer.
5. Top with ½ cup strawberry topping. To make strawberry topping, place 1 cup strawberries and 1 tsp apple juice concentrate in blender. Blend until smooth.

1 slice **Tofu Garden Quiche**
2 slices whole-wheat toast
1 Tbsp reduced-calorie margarine
½ cup mixed fresh fruit

Tofu Garden Quiche

Yield: 8 slices / Serving size: 1 slice

INGREDIENTS

2 tsp corn oil margarine
½ medium onion, finely chopped
2 cups cooked chopped vegetables (use a colorful assortment, such as red and green peppers and yellow squash)
2 eggs or ½ cup egg substitute

1 lb tofu, drained
1 Tbsp lemon juice
1 tsp dried oregano
1 tsp dried basil
½ tsp dried tarragon
¼ tsp salt
⅛ tsp garlic powder
⅛ tsp ground nutmeg
¼ cup Parmesan cheese

METHOD

1. Preheat oven to 325 degrees. Melt the margarine in a large skillet. Add onion and cook until onion is soft, about 5 minutes.
2. Add cooked vegetables and mix. Remove from heat and set aside.
3. Put eggs and half of the tofu into a blender and blend until smooth and creamy. Add remaining ingredients—except vegetable mixture and Parmesan cheese—and blend until smooth. Mix vegetables into tofu mixture.
4. Pour the tofu mixture into a large quiche dish or pie pan.
5. Sprinkle with Parmesan cheese.
6. Bake for 50 minutes to 1 hour or until knife comes out clean.

41

1 **Peanut Butter and Jelly Muffin**
1 cup nonfat fruit-flavored yogurt
½ grapefruit

Peanut Butter and Jelly Muffins

Yield: 12 muffins / Serving size: 1 muffin

INGREDIENTS

Nonstick vegetable cooking
   spray
2 cups flour
3 Tbsp sugar
1 Tbsp baking powder
¾ cup creamy peanut butter

1 egg
1 cup skim or 1% milk
⅓ cup no-sugar-added fruit
   spread (raspberry or
   strawberry)

METHOD

1. Preheat oven to 350 degrees.
2. Spray muffin tin with vegetable spray or line with baking cups.
3. In a large bowl, mix flour, sugar, and baking powder.
4. In another bowl, beat peanut butter and egg until smooth. Add milk a little at a time, stirring after each addition.
5. Pour peanut butter mixture over dry ingredients; fold in with a rubber spatula just until dry ingredients are moistened. Batter will be stiff.
6. Spoon 2 scant tablespoons of batter into each muffin cup and smooth the surface out to the top edge of the cup. Then top each muffin with a heaping teaspoon of fruit spread; cover with 2 more tablespoons of batter.
7. Bake 20–25 minutes or until lightly browned.

2 **Iowa Corn Pancakes** with
2 Tbsp sugar-free syrup and
1 Tbsp reduced-calorie margarine
¼ medium cantaloupe

Iowa Corn Pancakes

Yield: 8 pancakes / Serving size: 1 pancake

INGREDIENTS

1 cup sour skim or 1% milk (add 1 Tbsp white vinegar per
   1 cup milk)
½ cup rolled oats
1 cup whole-kernel corn (leftovers or canned can be used)
¼ cup all-purpose flour
¼ cup whole-wheat flour
¼ tsp salt
¾ tsp baking soda
¼ cup egg substitute
Nonstick vegetable cooking spray

METHOD

1. Combine milk, oats, and corn in a large mixing bowl
   and let stand for 8 minutes.
2. Mix flours, salt, and baking soda in a small bowl and set
   aside.
3. Add egg substitute to milk mixture and beat until
   blended.
4. Add dry ingredients to wet ingredients and stir until just
   mixed.
5. Pour slightly less than ⅓ cup batter on a hot griddle that
   has been sprayed with vegetable spray.
6. Cook until bubbles form on edges and edges start to dry.
7. Turn and cook 2–3 more minutes.

2 **Sweet Potato–Raisin Cookies**
1 cup skim or 1% milk

Sweet Potato–Raisin Cookies

Yield 24 cookies / Serving size: 2 cookies

INGREDIENTS

1 cup raisins
¼ cup butter or margarine
1 cup sweet potatoes,
  cooked and mashed
1 egg
1 tsp vanilla
2 cups whole-wheat flour
¼ tsp allspice
½ tsp salt

½ tsp nutmeg
½ tsp baking soda
1 tsp baking powder
1 tsp cinnamon
¼ cup walnuts, chopped
½ cup unprocessed bran
  flakes
Nonstick vegetable cooking
  spray

METHOD

1. Preheat oven to 350 degrees. Soak raisins in hot water to cover for 5 minutes, then drain.
2. Cream margarine, then add sweet potatoes, egg, and vanilla; beat until creamy.
3. Mix flour, allspice, salt, nutmeg, baking soda, baking powder, and cinnamon. Add to creamed mixture and mix well.
4. Add raisins, nuts, and bran.
5. Drop onto cookie sheet that has been sprayed with vegetable spray.
6. Bake for 12 minutes or until done.

1 serving **Baked Rice Pudding**
3 stewed prunes
2 Tbsp roasted almonds
1 cup skim or 1% milk

Baked Rice Pudding

Yield: 4 servings / Serving size: ⅖ cup

INGREDIENTS
1 cup skim or 1% milk
2 eggs, slightly beaten
1 Tbsp sugar
⅛ tsp salt
1 tsp vanilla
⅛ tsp grated nutmeg (optional)
2 cups cooked rice (or other whole grain)

METHOD
1. Preheat oven to 325 degrees.
2. Heat milk in the top of a double boiler over simmering water until surface begins to wrinkle.
3. Blend together eggs, sugar, salt, and vanilla. Add hot milk gradually, stirring to mix well.
4. Add rice. Pour into four 6-oz individual custard cups. Sprinkle surface lightly with nutmeg.
5. Set cups in a deep pan; pour hot water around cups to within ½ inch of tops of cups.
6. Bake 50–60 minutes or until toothpick comes out clean.
7. Remove from heat and water pan. Chill for several hours before serving.
8. Sprinkle with artificial sweetener, if desired.

45

1 serving **Low Country Grits and Sausage**
½ cup fresh citrus sections

Low Country Grits and Sausage

Yield: 2 servings / Serving size: ½ recipe

INGREDIENTS

2 oz turkey sausage
½ cup uncooked yellow or white grits (stone-ground are best)
2 eggs, beaten
½ cup skim or 1% milk
½ tsp thyme (optional)
⅛ tsp garlic salt (optional)
Nonstick vegetable cooking spray

METHOD

1. The night before, cook turkey sausage and crumble into small pieces.
2. Cook grits according to package directions.
3. Combine eggs, milk, thyme, and garlic salt in medium bowl. Add a small amount of hot grits and mix well. Add mixture to rest of grits.
4. Mix well and pour into a loaf pan that has been coated with vegetable spray. Cover and refrigerate overnight.
5. Next morning, remove from refrigerator and let stand 15 minutes before baking. Bake at 350 degrees for 45 minutes or until done.

1 slice **Johnnycake** with
1½ tsp reduced-calorie margarine
⅔ cup raspberries with
Artificial sweetener (optional)
1½ oz turkey ham
4 oz orange juice

Johnnycake

Yield: 1 loaf of 12 slices / Serving size: 1 slice

INGREDIENTS
2 cups cornmeal
1½ tsp salt
1 tsp baking soda
2 Tbsp sugar
2 cups buttermilk
½ cup egg substitute
2 Tbsp vegetable oil
Nonstick vegetable cooking spray

METHOD
1. Mix dry ingredients together.
2. Add buttermilk, egg substitute, and oil.
3. Mix well. Pour into 8- by 10-inch loaf pan coated with vegetable spray.
4. Bake in 400-degree oven for 30 minutes.

1 serving **Granola Pancakes**
3 tsp reduced-calorie margarine
3 Tbsp apple butter or ½ cup no-sugar-
    added applesauce

Granola Pancakes

Yield: About 18 4-inch pancakes / Serving size: 3 pancakes

INGREDIENTS
2 eggs or 1 egg plus 2 egg whites
2 cups skim or 1% milk
2 Tbsp molasses
2 cups whole-wheat flour
½ cup low-fat granola
2 tsp baking powder
Nonstick vegetable cooking spray

METHOD
1. Beat eggs in a large cup or bowl; add milk and molasses and stir.
2. Combine flour, granola, and baking powder and add to liquid mixture, mixing lightly with a fork.
3. Coat skillet with vegetable spray and heat over medium heat.
4. Drop pancake batter, using about ¼ cup per pancake, onto skillet. Turn pancakes once. Cook until golden brown on both sides.

Apple–Oat Bran Muffin

Yield: 24 muffins / Serving size: 1 muffin

INGREDIENTS
2 cups whole-wheat pastry flour
1½ cups oat bran
1¼ tsp baking soda
½ tsp nutmeg
1 Tbsp grated orange peel
1 cup chopped apples
½ cup raisins
2 cups buttermilk
1 beaten egg
⅓ cup dark molasses
2 Tbsp vegetable oil
Nonstick vegetable cooking spray

METHOD
1. Preheat oven to 350 degrees.
2. Toss flour, bran, baking soda, and nutmeg together.
3. Stir in grated orange rind, chopped apples, and raisins.
4. Add buttermilk, egg, molasses, and oil and stir with a few quick strokes.
5. Coat muffin tins with vegetable spray and fill two-thirds full with batter.
6. Bake 25 minutes.

1 serving **Oatmeal-Wheatena Porridge
With Banana and Walnuts**
½ cup skim or 1% milk

Oatmeal-Wheatena Porridge With Banana and Walnuts

Yield: 1 serving

INGREDIENTS
1 cup water
3 Tbsp Wheatena
¼ cup rolled oats
½ large banana, mashed
2 Tbsp chopped walnuts

METHOD
1. Add Wheatena and oats to boiling water. If using quick-cooking oats, allow Wheatena to cook a few minutes over moderate heat before adding oats.
2. Cook to desired consistency. Mix in the mashed banana.
3. Pour into bowl and top with chopped walnuts.

2 Whole-Wheat Currant Scones
1 cup low-fat artificially sweetened vanilla yogurt

Whole-Wheat Currant Scones

Yield: 16 scones / Serving size: 2 scones

INGREDIENTS

2 cups whole-wheat pastry flour
1 cup rolled oats
½ cup oat bran
2 Tbsp baking powder
¼ tsp salt
¼ tsp cream of tartar
4 Tbsp margarine

½ cup currants
⅔ cup nonfat plain yogurt
2 tsp vanilla extract
2 Tbsp orange juice
2 Tbsp sugar or fructose
½ cup egg substitute
Nonstick vegetable cooking spray

METHOD

1. Preheat oven to 425 degrees.
2. Mix flour, oats, oat bran, baking powder, salt, and cream of tartar in a bowl.
3. Cut in margarine until mixture is mealy. Add currants and mix until coated with flour.
4. In a small bowl, mix together yogurt, vanilla, orange juice, sugar, and egg substitute and add to dry ingredients, mixing just until a ball of dough forms. If mixture is too dry, add 1–2 Tbsp more yogurt.
5. Knead dough on floured pastry cloth about 10 times. Divide dough in half, and form two circles of dough about ½ inch thick.
6. Transfer to baking sheet coated with vegetable spray, and cut each circle into 8 pie-shaped wedges.
7. Bake for 12–15 minutes.

*L*unch

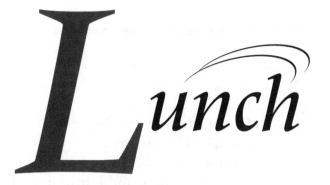

Each lunch in this section has about 450 calories and includes
2–3 Starch servings
1–2 Meat or Meat Substitute
      servings
0–2 Vegetable servings
1 Fruit serving
1 Fat serving

Total Fat: 15 grams

Total Carbohydrate: 50 grams

Protein: 22 grams

Some menus have 1 Skim Milk serving instead of 1 Meat or 1 Starch serving. Or 1 Starch serving instead of the Fruit serving.

No-Fuss Noons

1 cup vegetable soup
6 saltine crackers
½ Chicken Sandwich:
    1 slice whole-wheat bread
    2 oz chicken breast
    1 tsp mayonnaise
    Lettuce, tomato, and mustard, as desired
1 orange or ⅓ cup frozen yogurt

2 oz lean ham
⅓ cup cooked white or yellow rice
⅓ cup black beans with
1 tsp olive oil and
Chopped onion and
Vinegar to taste
½ cup turnip greens with
Hot pepper sauce to taste
2 figs

LUNCH

Chef Salad:
    2 cups lettuce
    Chopped raw vegetables
    1 oz ham, turkey, or chicken
    1 oz cheese
    2 tomato wedges
    2 Tbsp reduced-calorie dressing
3 RyKrisp crackers
1¼ cups strawberries
3 oz frozen low-fat yogurt

Reuben Sandwich:
    2 slices toasted rye bread
    1 oz cooked corned beef, sliced
    ¾ oz mozzarella cheese, sliced
    1 Tbsp reduced-calorie Thousand Island
        dressing
    ¼ cup sauerkraut
½ cup pears canned in water

Build sandwich, wrap in microwave-safe paper towel, and microwave for 15 seconds or until heated.

1 10¾-oz can chunky vegetable soup
1 slice whole-wheat toast with
1 oz melted Monterey Jack cheese
15 grapes

Macaroni Salad:
- 1 cup cooked macaroni, drained and chilled
- 2 oz part-skim mozzarella cheese cubes
- 2 Tbsp chopped green pepper
- 2 Tbsp chopped carrots
- 2 Tbsp chopped onions
- 1 Tbsp low-fat mayonnaise
- 1 Tbsp nonfat artificially sweetened plain yogurt

1 kiwifruit

1 Vegetable-Topped Potato:
- 8-oz baking potato, microwaved, topped with
- ¼ cup low-fat cottage cheese
- 2 Tbsp grated cheddar cheese
- ¼ cup broccoli florets
- ¼ cup chopped tomato
- ¼ cup chopped green onions
- ¼ cup sliced mushrooms

⅓ cup frozen yogurt

1 medium apple

Stouffer's Lean Cuisine Cheese Cannelloni
with Tomato Sauce
½ cup steamed broccoli with
1 tsp margarine
2 bread sticks
1 cup mixed berries (strawberries,
raspberries, or blueberries)

Pasta Salad:
1 cup pasta, cooked
¼ cup water-packed canned tuna,
drained
1 oz cheddar cheese, shredded
1 cup mixture of broccoli, cucumber, and
green, red, or yellow peppers
2 Tbsp reduced-calorie dressing
1 small tomato, cut into wedges
1 medium nectarine

1 energy bar
3 cups air-popped (fat-free) popcorn
2 tubes (2 oz total) string cheese
1 cup carrot sticks
2 dried apple rings

Olive-Tuna Salad:
  2 cups torn lettuce with
  ½ cup water-packed canned tuna,
    drained
  1 chopped tomato
  ½ cup new potatoes, boiled, chopped,
    and chilled
  5 small black, green, or Greek olives
  2–3 Tbsp fat-free dressing
6 saltine crackers
1 small pear

1 Kentucky Fried Chicken skinless center
  breast
1 ear corn on the cob
1 medium apple
1 serving coleslaw

This menu is 1 Fat exchange over the lunch allowance and is for occasional use only. Try to balance this meal with less fat in the other meals that day.

Quesadillas:
Nonstick vegetable cooking spray
2 6-inch flour tortillas
2 oz reduced-fat cheddar cheese, grated
¼ cup salsa
1 cup carrot sticks

Coat skillet with vegetable spray, then heat. Put 1 tortilla in pan and sprinkle with grated cheese. Cover with second tortilla. Brown on both sides. Dip in salsa.

⅔ cup canned kidney beans warmed up with
Finely diced onion, garlic, and green pepper to taste
¼ cup tomato sauce with
Cajun seasoning to taste over
½ cup cooked brown rice
Tossed green salad with
2 Tbsp reduced-calorie ranch dressing

1 Salmon Pita Pocket Sandwich:
    1 6-inch whole-wheat pita pocket
    ½ cup canned salmon, drained, with
    1 Tbsp low-fat mayonnaise
    ½ cup shredded lettuce
    2 tomato slices
1¼ cups watermelon cubes

Stuffed Baked Potato:
    1 medium baked potato topped with
    2 oz American cheese and
    ¼ cup chopped raw or cooked broccoli
1 nectarine

8 RyKrisp crackers
Shrimp Salad:
    4 oz shrimp
    Bed of lettuce and fresh raw vegetables,
      as desired
    1 chopped tomato
    ⅛ avocado with
    2 Tbsp **French Dressing**
    ½ cup grapefruit sections

French Dressing

Yield: 6 servings / Serving size: 2 Tbsp

INGREDIENTS

½ cup tomato juice
2 Tbsp lemon juice or vinegar
1 Tbsp finely chopped onion
1 Tbsp finely chopped green pepper
¼ tsp salt
⅛ tsp black pepper

METHOD

1. Combine all ingredients in jar. Cover and shake well
   before using.

1 slice **Whole-Wheat Pizza**
Tossed salad with
1 Tbsp Italian dressing
⅛ honeydew melon

Whole-Wheat Pizza

Yield: 8 servings / Serving size: 1 slice

INGREDIENTS

1 cup warm water
  (110–115 degrees)
1 pkg. (or 1 Tbsp) active dry
  yeast or 1 cake yeast
1 Tbsp honey
2¼–2½ cups whole-wheat
  flour
½ tsp salt
1 Tbsp vegetable oil
4 oz cheddar cheese, grated
½ tsp pepper

½ tsp caraway seeds
¼ tsp garlic powder
½ cup tomato sauce or pizza
  sauce
½–1 Tbsp dried oregano
1 cup broccoli pieces
1 cup zucchini slices
1 cup mushroom slices
8 oz part-skim mozzarella
  cheese, shredded

METHOD

1. Combine water, yeast, honey, and 1 cup of whole-wheat flour in a large bowl. Beat 100 times until mixture is smooth. Let rise in a warm place for 15 minutes.
2. Add salt, oil, cheddar cheese, pepper, caraway seeds, garlic powder, and 1¼–1½ cups whole-wheat flour.
3. Mix well and let the dough rest for 5 minutes.
4. Pat out dough onto a baking sheet for 1 large pizza, or divide the dough in half and make 2 medium-sized pizzas.
5. Top with the pizza sauce, oregano, vegetables, and mozzarella.
6. Bake in a 400-degree oven for 15–20 minutes.

1 cup **Noodle Supreme Salad**
5 Triscuit crackers with
1 tsp margarine
1 apple

Noodle Supreme Salad

Yield: 2 servings / Serving size: 1 cup

INGREDIENTS

2 oz noodles
¼ cup frozen peas
3 cups water
3 Tbsp cream of mushroom soup
2 oz water-packed canned tuna, drained
2 Tbsp shredded red cabbage
¼ cup diced tomatoes
⅛ tsp salt
Pinch of pepper
Lettuce leaf
Green onion, chopped, if desired

METHOD

1. Bring water to a boil. Add noodles and peas. Cook uncovered 5 minutes. Drain.
2. Combine noodles, peas, soup, and tuna. Mix lightly. Cool.
3. Add red cabbage and tomatoes. Sprinkle with salt and pepper.
4. Serve on lettuce leaf and garnish with chopped green onion.

LUNCH

1 cup **Black Bean Soup**
6 saltine crackers
Tossed salad with
2 Tbsp reduced-calorie dressing
½ cup canned no-sugar-added fruit cocktail

Black Bean Soup

Yield: 4 servings / Serving size: 1 cup

INGREDIENTS

½ lb dried black beans
1 qt water
1½ tsp salt (optional)
1 Tbsp olive oil
1 cup chopped onions
½ cup chopped green
    pepper (optional)

1 tsp minced garlic
½ tsp ground cumin
½ tsp oregano
⅛ tsp dry mustard
1½ tsp lemon juice
Green onions, chopped
    (optional)

METHOD

1. Presoak beans in water overnight or use quick-cook method on package.
2. After soaking beans, add 1 tsp salt and bring to a boil; cover and simmer on low heat for 2 hours.
3. Heat oil, add onions, and sauté about 5 minutes. Add green pepper and sauté until onions are tender.
4. Stir in remaining ingredients. Add about ¾ cup hot bean liquid, cover, and simmer 10 minutes.
5. Add onion seasoning mixture to beans and continue to cook 1 hour, stirring occasionally.
6. To serve, top with chopped green onions, if desired.

1 **Sloppy Joe** on
Hamburger bun
Raw carrot and celery sticks
1 apple
4 vanilla wafers

Sloppy Joes

Yield: 6 servings / Serving size: ½ cup

INGREDIENTS
1 lb ground beef
½ cup chopped onion
½ cup chopped celery
1 8-oz can tomato sauce
½ tsp salt
Dash pepper
6 hamburger buns (about 2 oz each)

METHOD
1. Sauté ground beef, onion, and celery. Drain excess fat.
2. Add remaining ingredients. Simmer 10 minutes.
3. Spoon onto hamburger buns, allowing scant ½ cup per bun.

LUNCH

1 cup chicken noodle soup
1 **English Muffin Pizza Melt**
Tossed salad with
2 Tbsp reduced-calorie dressing
1 pear

English Muffin Pizza Melt

Yield: 6 servings / Serving size: ½ muffin plus ⅙ topping

INGREDIENTS

1 lb lean ground beef
¼ cup onion, chopped
Nonstick vegetable cooking spray
1 8-oz can pizza sauce
1 tsp dried parsley flakes
½ tsp basil
¼ tsp garlic powder
2 Tbsp mozzarella cheese, shredded
3 English muffins, split

METHOD

1. Preheat oven to 350 degrees.
2. Cook beef and onion in skillet coated with vegetable spray. Cook until meat is no longer pink. Drain and dry with paper towels to reduce fat. Stir in pizza sauce and seasonings.
3. Top each muffin with ⅙ cup beef mixture. You may toast muffins before adding meat and cheese. Top with 1 tsp cheese.
4. Place in oven and bake for 10–15 minutes or until heated thoroughly and cheese is melted.

1 Tortilla Ranch Style
1 medium nectarine

23

Tortilla Ranch Style

Yield: 1 serving

INGREDIENTS

1 cup assorted vegetables (carrots, celery, zucchini, green
   onions, spinach, sweet red peppers, and/or lettuce),
   thinly shredded
1 large flour tortilla
2 Tbsp reduced-calorie ranch dressing
1 oz Swiss cheese
1 oz sliced turkey

METHOD

1. Layer vegetables on tortilla.
2. Sprinkle dressing over vegetables.
3. Add Swiss cheese and turkey. Roll up. Eat cold or
   microwave briefly.

LUNCH

1 Submarine Sandwich
1 oz pretzel rings
1 medium pear

Submarine Sandwich

Yield: 4 sandwiches / Serving size: 1 sandwich

INGREDIENTS
½ loaf (½ lb) French bread
½ Tbsp mustard, or to taste
2 oz part-skim mozzarella cheese, sliced
¼ lb turkey, sliced
1 cup shredded lettuce
1 medium tomato, thinly sliced
½ medium onion, thinly sliced
2 oz fully cooked smoked ham, thinly sliced
½ medium green pepper, thinly sliced
2 Tbsp low-calorie Italian dressing
4 long wooden picks or small skewers

METHOD
1. Cut bread into halves horizontally. Spread bottom half with mustard.
2. Layer cheese, turkey, lettuce, tomatoes, onion, ham, and green pepper on top. Drizzle with dressing; top with remaining bread half. Secure loaf with picks. To serve, cut into 4 pieces.

25

1 cup **Minestrone**
4 RyKrisp crackers
2 oz part-skim mozzarella cheese
1¼ cups strawberries

Minestrone

Yield: 5 servings / Serving size: 1 cup

INGREDIENTS

½ cup chopped onion
1½ cloves garlic, chopped
1½ tsp olive oil
1 qt beef broth
½ cup sliced zucchini
⅓ cup chopped carrot
1 rib celery, chopped
14 oz canned Italian plum tomatoes
1 19-oz can cannelloni beans, or any type of white cooked bean, drained

½ cup shredded cabbage
½ cup peeled and cubed potato
½ tsp basil
¼ tsp black pepper
1 Tbsp tomato paste
½ 10-oz pkg. frozen Italian-cut string beans
¼ cup elbow macaroni
¼ cup Parmesan cheese

METHOD

1. In large stock pot, sauté onion and garlic in olive oil until soft but not brown (about 10 minutes). Add remaining ingredients, except Italian green beans, pasta, and Parmesan cheese.
2. Bring to a boil, cover, reduce heat, and simmer for 1 hour.
3. Stir in beans, pasta, and half the Parmesan cheese. Simmer for an additional 15 minutes.
4. Season to taste. Serve hot or at room temperature with remaining Parmesan cheese.

1 serving **Spicy Black-Eyed Peas**
3 oz hamburger patty
Tossed salad with
1 Tbsp cheddar cheese, grated
1 medium orange

Spicy Black-Eyed Peas

Yield: 4 servings / Serving size: 1¼ cups

INGREDIENTS
Nonstick vegetable cooking spray
½ cup chopped onion
½ cup chopped green pepper
1 16-oz can black-eyed peas, undrained
1 16-oz can stewed tomatoes, undrained
1 tsp dry mustard
½ tsp chili powder
⅛ tsp red pepper
½ tsp pepper
1 Tbsp soy sauce
1 tsp liquid smoke
1 Tbsp minced fresh parsley

METHOD
1. Coat a large nonstick skillet with cooking spray; place over medium heat until hot.
2. Add onion and green pepper; sauté until vegetables are tender-crisp.
3. Add peas and next 7 ingredients; bring to a boil. Reduce heat; simmer 20 minutes, stirring often. Transfer to a serving dish. Sprinkle with parsley.

27

1 serving **Crunchy Tuna Cheese Melt**
1 cup vegetable soup
4 apricot halves, unsweetened

Crunchy Tuna Cheese Melt

Yield: 1 serving / Serving size: 2 slices

INGREDIENTS

½ cup water-packed canned tuna, drained
2 Tbsp nonfat artificially sweetened plain yogurt
4 water chestnuts, sliced
2 Tbsp chopped onion
2 Tbsp chopped celery
2 slices whole-wheat bread, toasted
¼ cup shredded Monterey Jack cheese
2 green pepper rings

METHOD

1. In small bowl, combine tuna, yogurt, water chestnuts, onions, and celery.
2. Spread on toasted bread. Top with shredded cheese and broil until cheese melts. Garnish each slice with a green pepper ring.

1 serving **Fast Corn Chowder**
6 saltine crackers
¼ cup low-fat cottage cheese on lettuce leaf
1 cup melon balls

Fast Corn Chowder

Yield: 4 servings / Serving size: 1 cup

INGREDIENTS

1 17-oz can cream-style corn
1 12-oz can whole kernel corn with sweet peppers, undrained
1 12-oz can or 1½ cups evaporated skim milk
1 tsp dried minced onion
Dash pepper
1 Tbsp margarine

METHOD

1. In a medium saucepan, combine both cans of corn, evaporated milk, onion, and pepper.
2. Bring to a boil, stirring constantly. Add margarine. Serve.

New Potato–Veggie Pizza
Tossed green salad with
1 Tbsp fat-free dressing
¼ cantaloupe

New Potato–Veggie Pizza

Yield: 1 serving

INGREDIENTS

Nonstick vegetable cooking spray
2 medium new potatoes (6 oz total weight), washed and
   sliced ⅛ inch thick
2 Tbsp water
1 tsp olive oil
¼ cup spaghetti sauce
1 small clove garlic, crushed
¼ tsp Italian seasonings
¼ green pepper, sliced
⅛ small red onion, sliced
⅓ cup thinly sliced zucchini
1 oz mozzarella cheese, shredded

METHOD

1. Coat nonstick 8- or 10-inch skillet with vegetable spray.
   Spread potatoes on the bottom and add water and oil.
   Cover and cook until just tender.
2. Uncover and raise heat to evaporate water. Brown on
   one side and then flip potatoes over in one piece. Lower
   heat.
3. Mix spaghetti sauce with garlic and seasonings. Spread
   sauce on top of potatoes.
4. Top with sliced vegetables and then cheese. Raise heat
   to medium and cook covered until potatoes are browned
   and vegetables are cooked.

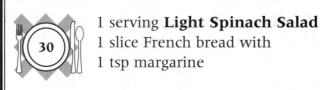

1 serving **Light Spinach Salad**
1 slice French bread with
1 tsp margarine

Light Spinach Salad

Yield: 2 servings / Serving size: ½ recipe

INGREDIENTS

4 cups torn fresh spinach
4 oz cooked skinless breast of chicken, cubed
1 medium orange, peeled, seeded, and sectioned
½ cup sliced mushrooms
1 small onion, sliced
2 oz cheddar cheese, cubed or in strips
2 Tbsp reduced-calorie dressing

METHOD

1. Combine all ingredients except cheese and dressing in a large bowl; chill.
2. Before serving, add cheese and toss with dressing.

1 serving **Gazpacho**
2 slices whole-wheat bread
½ cup egg salad made with
1 Tbsp low-fat mayonnaise
1 medium nectarine

Gazpacho

Yield: 4 servings / Serving size: 1 cup

INGREDIENTS
4 medium tomatoes, quartered
1 small cucumber, peeled and sliced
¼ cup sliced onion
2 stalks celery, quartered
½ green pepper, sliced
1 clove garlic, minced
1 tsp salt
¼ tsp pepper
2 Tbsp vegetable oil
3 Tbsp wine vinegar
½ cup V-8 juice

METHOD
1. Core and remove seeds from 1 tomato. Chop finely; set aside.
2. Combine all other ingredients in blender container. Blend only a few seconds. Mixture should not be smooth.
3. Add chopped tomato. Chill.
4. Serve in chilled bowls with an ice cube in each serving.

1 Broiled Open-Faced Vegetarian Sandwich
1 small banana

32

Broiled Open-Faced Vegetarian Sandwich

Yield: 1 serving

INGREDIENTS

2 slices Italian Bread, 1 inch thick
2 tsp reduced-calorie margarine
Tomato slices
Zucchini slices
Onion slices
Green pepper slices
Garlic powder
Basil
Pepper
2 oz part-skim mozzarella cheese

METHOD

1. Spread bread with 1 tsp margarine on each.
2. Top with tomato, zucchini, onion, and green pepper slices.
3. Sprinkle with garlic powder, basil, and pepper; top with cheese.
4. Broil until browned on edges and cheese is melted.

1 slice cold **Spicy Turkey Loaf**

2 slices reduced-calorie bread (40 calories each)

Lettuce and tomato slice or ketchup, as desired

½ mango or 12 cherries

Spicy Turkey Loaf

Yield: 8 servings / Serving size: 1 slice

INGREDIENTS

1½ lb ground turkey

¾ cup evaporated milk

¼ cup finely chopped onion

1 cup bread crumbs

4 Tbsp chili sauce

½ tsp ground ginger

½ tsp crushed fresh garlic clove

A few parsley or cilantro leaves, chopped

METHOD

1. Preheat oven to 350 degrees.
2. Mix all ingredients together. Press into an ungreased loaf pan.
3. Bake 45 minutes or until toothpick comes out clean. Cool about 5 minutes, then cut into 8 slices.

2 Pizza Muffins
Tossed salad with
2 Tbsp reduced-calorie dressing
1 apple

Pizza Muffins

Yield: 12 muffins / Serving size: 2 muffins

INGREDIENTS

Nonstick vegetable cooking
   spray
1 egg
½ cup tomato sauce
1 cup buttermilk or low-fat
   plain yogurt
1 tsp oregano
¼ tsp garlic powder
¼ tsp freshly ground pepper

4 oz mozzarella cheese,
   diced
1½ cups whole-wheat flour
3 Tbsp wheat germ
2 tsp baking powder
1 tsp baking soda
Sliced tomatoes and sesame
   seeds for garnish

METHOD

1. Preheat oven to 400 degrees. Spray muffin tin with vegetable spray or line with baking cups.
2. Blend egg, tomato sauce, and buttermilk with a mixer or food processor. Add spices. Add cheese, reserving ¼ cup for topping.
3. In another bowl, mix flour, wheat germ, baking powder, and baking soda.
4. Combine the two mixtures until flour is no longer visible. Spoon batter into muffin tin, filling each well about two-thirds full. Top each muffin with a slice of tomato and some cheese; sprinkle with sesame seeds.
5. Bake 20–25 minutes.

1 serving **Fiesta Rice**
½ cup green beans
3 medium prunes
Tossed salad
1 Tbsp creamy ranch dressing

Fiesta Rice

Yield: 4 servings / Serving size: 1 cup

INGREDIENTS
2½ cups cooked brown rice
¾ cup low-fat cottage cheese
1 cup grated reduced-fat cheddar cheese
2-oz jar pimentos, drained and chopped
½ cup skim or 1% milk
1 large tomato, peeled and diced
Dash paprika
Nonstick vegetable cooking spray

METHOD
1. Preheat oven to 350 degrees.
2. Combine ½ cup of cheddar cheese and all other ingredients except paprika. Stir until well mixed.
3. Spray casserole with vegetable spray.
4. Pour in mixture; top with remaining cheddar cheese and sprinkle well with paprika.
5. Bake 25–30 minutes.

LUNCH

Squash Casserole

Yield: 6 servings / Serving size: ⅙ recipe

INGREDIENTS

1 medium onion, chopped
2 Tbsp margarine
1½ lb yellow squash, sliced
1 cup shredded carrots
3 cups Pepperidge Farm stuffing mix
1 cup low-fat sour cream
1 egg
1 cup chicken broth or enough to moisten
12 oz skinless turkey breast, cubed
Nonstick vegetable cooking spray

METHOD

1. Preheat oven to 375 degrees.
2. Sauté onion in margarine. Mix with remaining ingredients.
4. Pour into 2-qt baking dish coated with vegetable spray.
5. Bake 30–40 minutes or until bubbly.

	1 serving **Pan-Broiled Shrimp**
37	1 medium tomato, sliced
	1 cup cooked stone-ground grits
	¾ cup fresh pineapple

Pan-Broiled Shrimp

Yield: 3 servings / Serving size: ⅓ recipe

INGREDIENTS

1 tsp margarine
⅓ medium sweet onion, sliced
⅓ lb shrimp, peeled and deveined
Lemon juice, salt, and pepper to taste

METHOD

1. Heat margarine in medium saucepan. Sauté onion until translucent.
2. Add shrimp. Sauté until pink, about 3–5 minutes.
3. Add lemon juice, salt, and pepper to taste.

1 cup **Spanish Garbanzo Beans**
½ cup sliced cucumbers in red wine vinegar
½ cup grapes

Spanish Garbanzo Beans

Yield: 2 servings / Serving size: 1 cup

INGREDIENTS

½ cup chopped onions
1 medium green pepper, chopped
2 Tbsp olive oil
8 oz tomato sauce
1¼ cups cooked garbanzo beans

METHOD

1. Sauté onions and pepper in olive oil. Add tomato sauce. Cook over medium heat for 5 minutes.
2. Add garbanzo beans. Cook over low heat for 15 minutes.

1 serving **Schinkennudelin**
1 slice bread
1 cup sliced cucumbers with
1 Tbsp reduced-calorie creamy cucumber
dressing
15 grapes

Schinkennudelin

Yield: 1 serving

INGREDIENTS
1 oz low-fat ham, cubed
1 Tbsp reduced-calorie margarine
½ cup cooked noodles
1 egg, beaten

METHOD
1. Brown ham cubes in margarine.
2. Add noodles and brown.
3. Add beaten egg and continue to brown by turning in sections.

1 serving **Lentil-Veggie Soup**
Green salad with
2 Tbsp reduced-calorie dressing
1 orange

Lentil-Veggie Soup

Yield: 4 servings / Serving size: 1½ cups

INGREDIENTS

2 cups dried lentils
1 Tbsp salt
¼ cup vegetable oil
2 large carrots, sliced
1 large onion, diced
1 clove garlic, minced
¾ cup celery, chopped
1 10-oz pkg. frozen spinach, thawed
6 oz turkey ham, cubed

METHOD

1. Wash lentils. Soak overnight in generous amount of water.
2. Add salt and oil to water before soaking. Do not reduce salt or oil because foaming may result, causing a safety hazard in your pressure cooker. Most of the salt and oil will run off when lentils are drained.
3. Drain lentils.
4. Combine all ingredients in pressure cooker and add water to cover by 2 inches.
5. Close cover securely. Place pressure regulator on vent pipe and cook for 18 minutes after pressure is achieved.
6. Allow pressure to drop of its own accord.
7. In no case should the contents of the pressure cooker pass the maximum capacity line. Refer to your owner's manual for explanation. Recipe may be halved.

41

1 serving **Seven-Layer Salad**
2 pieces Wasa Crisp Bread
1 medium Granny Smith apple

Seven-Layer Salad

Yield: 2 servings / Serving size: ½ recipe

INGREDIENTS

3 cups torn iceberg lettuce
1 cup frozen green peas, thawed
¼ cup chopped onions
½ cup chopped celery
¼ cup chopped green pepper
¼ cup nonfat plain yogurt
2 Tbsp low-fat mayonnaise
2 oz reduced-fat cheddar cheese
2 slices bacon, cooked crisp, drained, and crumbled
2 hard-boiled eggs, sliced

METHOD

1. In a medium casserole dish, layer lettuce and other vegetables.
2. Mix together yogurt and mayonnaise and spread on the top layer. Top with cheese, bacon, and eggs.
3. Cover with plastic wrap and refrigerate 8 hours or more.

LUNCH

1 serving **Caesar Salad**
1 cup frozen melon balls (half cantaloupe, half honeydew)

Caesar Salad

Yield: 2 servings / Serving size: ½ recipe

INGREDIENTS

1 medium head romaine lettuce
Dressing:
    1 clove garlic, crushed
    ½ tsp black pepper
    2 oz smoked anchovies, drained and patted dry
    1 egg yolk, hard boiled
    4 Tbsp lemon juice
    2 Tbsp balsamic vinegar
    1 tsp Dijon mustard, prepared
    1 tsp Worcestershire sauce
    2 Tbsp olive oil
    ⅓ cup Parmesan cheese
Croutons:
    4 1-oz slices Italian bread, cubed
    2 tsp olive oil
    1 clove garlic, halved
    1 Tbsp chopped fresh parsley

1. Crisp lettuce by separating leaves and rinsing well under cold water. Pat dry with paper towels and break into 2-inch pieces. Roll in clean paper towels, place in plastic bag, and seal. Refrigerate until cold and well crisped, about 1 hour.
2. For dressing, combine garlic, pepper, and anchovies in a blender. At high speed, blend until garlic and anchovies are finely chopped. Add egg yolk, lemon juice, vinegar, mustard, and Worcestershire sauce. Blend until mixture is smooth.
3. Turn blender on high and, with machine running, remove center of lid or lid itself. Slowly pour olive oil in a thin, steady stream. Blend until all oil is added and dressing is smooth and creamy. Set aside or refrigerate until ready to add to salad. Do not leave unrefrigerated for more than 1 hour.
4. For croutons, heat olive oil and garlic in medium skillet until oil is hot and garlic is fragrant. Remove pan from heat and cool to room temperature. Discard garlic.
5. Add bread cubes and toss to coat. Sauté over medium-high heat until golden brown. Cool.
6. To build salad, place crisp lettuce pieces in a medium bowl. Pour dressing over salad and sprinkle with grated Parmesan cheese and croutons. Mix.

LUNCH

1 serving **Pintos and Potatoes**
1 cup **Mastokhiar** (page 87)

Pintos and Potatoes

Yield: 6 servings / Serving size: ⅙ recipe

INGREDIENTS

1½ cups dried pinto beans
½ tsp salt (optional)
1 potato, peeled and sliced
2 Tbsp lemon juice
2 Tbsp olive oil

METHOD

1. Wash and rinse beans well. Soak beans overnight in enough water to cover.
2. Drain beans and rinse again. Put beans in slow cooker or saucepan and add water to cover by at least 2 inches. Add salt.
3. If using a slow cooker, also add the sliced potato and cook on low for about 12 hours.
4. If cooking on stovetop, simmer until beans are almost tender, about 2 hours, then add sliced potato. Simmer another 45 minutes.
5. Add lemon juice and oil when serving.

Mastokhiar

Yield: 2 servings / Serving size: 1 cup

INGREDIENTS
1½ cups low-fat plain yogurt
1 cucumber, peeled and finely chopped
¼ cup raisins
⅛ tsp salt
½ tsp dried or ½ Tbsp chopped fresh mint leaves

METHOD
1. Mix all ingredients. Chill 1–2 hours before serving.

1 serving **Shrimp and Pea Salad**
2 4-inch bread sticks
1 slice **Low-Fat Lemon Cheesecake**
(page 89)

Shrimp and Pea Salad

Yield: 4 servings / Serving size: ¼ recipe

INGREDIENTS

1 16-oz pkg. frozen peas, thawed
1 tsp dill weed
¼ cup chopped red onion
1 cup cooked shrimp, peeled and deveined
2 Tbsp nonfat mayonnaise
½ cup low-fat plain yogurt

METHOD

1. Mix all ingredients together.

Low-Fat Lemon Cheesecake

Yield: 16 slices / Serving size: 1 slice

INGREDIENTS

Nonstick vegetable cooking spray
1/4 cup graham cracker crumbs
16 oz low-fat cream cheese
1 cup sugar
2/3 cup egg substitute
1 3/4–2 cups plain yogurt cheese (yogurt drained in
    cheesecloth until semisolid)
2 tsp vanilla
1 tsp grated lemon peel
1 Tbsp lemon juice
Sliced oranges, strawberries, and/or kiwifruit for garnish

METHOD

1. Heat oven to 350 degrees. Coat a 9-inch springform pan
   with vegetable spray and sprinkle bottom with graham
   cracker crumbs. Refrigerate.
2. In a large bowl, beat cream cheese until smooth.
   Gradually add sugar, beating until smooth. Add
   remaining ingredients except fruit and beat until smooth.
   Pour into pan.
3. Bake 50–60 minutes or until edges are set. (To minimize
   cracking, place a shallow pan half full of hot water on
   lower oven rack while baking.)
4. Remove from oven and cool on a wire rack. Remove
   sides of pan and refrigerate 6 hours or overnight. Top
   with fruit just before serving.

LUNCH

1 cup **Southwestern Veggie Soup**
1 Banana Smoothie:
　½ banana
　1 cup skim or 1% milk

Slice peeled banana, place in blender, add milk, then blend until smooth.

Southwestern Veggie Soup

Yield: 4 servings / Serving size: 1 cup

INGREDIENTS

2 corn tortillas
Nonstick vegetable cooking spray
½ tsp vegetable oil
⅓ cup chopped onion
⅓ cup chopped green pepper
1 clove garlic, crushed
1½ cups frozen corn
1 medium tomato, chopped
2 cups water
⅓ tsp beef or vegetable bouillon
¼ tsp oregano
1 tsp cornstarch mixed with 1 Tbsp cold water
1 Tbsp chopped fresh cilantro or parsley leaves
¼ cup mild salsa
1 cup canned pinto beans
1 cup shredded mozzarella cheese
⅛ tsp thyme

METHOD

1. Cut tortillas into eighths.
2. Coat nonstick cookie sheet with vegetable spray.
3. Toast tortillas on cookie sheet at 400 degrees for 10 minutes or until crisp.
4. Sauté vegetables in vegetable oil for 2–3 minutes.
5. Add water, bouillon, oregano, cornstarch paste, cilantro, salsa, and beans and let simmer for 5 minutes.
6. Ladle soup into 4 shallow bowls. Distribute toasted tortilla pieces equally between the bowls.
7. Top each bowl with ¼ cup shredded cheese and a pinch of thyme.

LUNCH

½ cup **Hummus**
1 7-inch whole-wheat pita
1 cup shredded lettuce
1 cup green pepper and tomato salad with
1 Tbsp reduced-calorie dressing
1 cup cubed watermelon

Hummus

Yield: 2 cups / Serving size: ½ cup

INGREDIENTS

2 cups cooked garbanzo beans, drained (½ cup juice
   reserved)
1 clove garlic
1 Tbsp sesame tahini
2 Tbsp olive oil
⅛ tsp salt (optional)
1 Tbsp lemon juice

METHOD

1. Blend all ingredients in a blender or food processor.

47

1 serving **Cucumbers With Dill Dressing**
1 cup Progresso Healthy Classics lentil soup
3 RyKrisp crackers
2 Tbsp peanuts mixed with
2 Tbsp raisins

Cucumbers With Dill Dressing

Yield: 3 servings / Serving size: ¾ cup

INGREDIENTS

Dressing:
  2 Tbsp wine vinegar
  1 Tbsp vegetable oil
  ½ tsp sugar
  ¼ tsp salt (optional)
  ¼ tsp dried dill
  ⅛ tsp pepper (optional)
1 cup cucumber slices, ⅛ inch thick
1 cup thinly sliced red onion in rings (optional)
1 medium tomato cut into wedges

METHOD

1. Combine dressing ingredients in a large bowl.
2. Add vegetables and mix to coat with dressing.
3. Let stand 15 minutes before serving.

1 serving **Bean Salad**
2 **Whole-Grain Muffins** (page 95)
1 oz low-fat mozzarella cheese
½ cup mixed pineapple and kiwifruit slices

48

Bean Salad

Yield: 6 servings / Serving size: 1 cup

LUNCH

INGREDIENTS

1½ cups fresh green beans
1½ cups fresh yellow beans
1½ cups cooked kidney beans
1 cup chopped green peppers
½ cup sliced onions
1 clove garlic, minced
⅔ cup red wine vinegar
6 pkgs. artificial sweetener
¼ cup olive oil
½ tsp Worcestershire sauce

METHOD

1. Blanch green and yellow beans. Cool. Mix with kidney beans, peppers, and onions.
2. Mix remaining ingredients and toss with beans. Let stand 1 hour before serving.

Whole-Grain Muffins

Yield: 10–12 muffins / Serving size: 1 muffin

INGREDIENTS
1 cup whole-wheat flour
1 tsp baking powder
½ tsp salt
1 Tbsp safflower oil
1 egg, beaten
1 cup buttermilk
1 Tbsp molasses

METHOD
1. Preheat oven to 450 degrees.
2. Mix together dry ingredients. Work in oil with a pastry blender.
3. Add egg, buttermilk, and molasses and stir well.
4. Fill lightly greased muffin tins a little more than half full. Bake for 17 minutes. Serve hot.

LUNCH

½ cup **Spiced Tomato Juice**
1 serving **Spaghetti Salad** (page 97)
¼ cup fat-free cottage cheese
8 whole-grain crackers
¾ cup fresh pineapple chunks

Spiced Tomato Juice

Yield: 8 servings / Serving size: ½ cup

INGREDIENTS

1 46-oz can low-sodium tomato juice
½ tsp onion powder
½ tsp celery seed
½ tsp dried basil
2 Tbsp artificial sweetener
2 Tbsp wine vinegar
Tabasco to taste

METHOD

1. Mix all ingredients together well and chill.

Spaghetti Salad

Yield: 8 servings / Serving size: ½ cup

INGREDIENTS

1 8-oz box whole-wheat spaghetti
8 oz fat-free Italian dressing
½ cup sliced fresh mushrooms
½ cup chopped green peppers
½ cup chopped onions
Cherry tomatoes (optional)

METHOD

1. Cook spaghetti according to package directions. Drain.
2. Combine spaghetti, dressing, mushrooms, peppers, onions, and tomatoes. Refrigerate.

LUNCH

Grated Carrot–Raisin Salad
1 cup pea soup
1 small (1-oz) whole-grain roll with
1 Tbsp sesame tahini

Grated Carrot–Raisin Salad

Yield: 1 serving

INGREDIENTS

1 medium-sized carrot
2 Tbsp raisins
1 Tbsp lemon juice
Artificial sweetener to taste

METHOD

1. Wash and peel carrot. Finely grate carrot in food processor or hand grater.
2. Add lemon juice and raisins. Mix well into carrots.
3. Sprinkle sweetener over salad to taste and combine well.

Dinner

Each dinner in this section has about 550 calories and includes
2–3 Starch servings
1–3 Meat or Meat Substitute
    servings
1–3 Vegetable servings
1 Fruit serving
1–2 Fat servings

Total Fat: 20 grams

Total Carbohydrate: 45 grams

Protein: 33 grams

Some menus have 1 Skim Milk serving instead of 1 Meat, 1 Starch, or 1 Fruit serving.

No-Fuss Evenings

Stouffer's Macaroni and Cheese (11½-oz
    pkg.)
1 cup steamed broccoli
Peach melba parfait:
    1 fresh peach, sliced, or ½ cup water-
        packed canned peaches
    2 Tbsp Raspberry Sauce (page 144)

*Note: Macaroni and cheese is high in saturated fat and sodium
and is for occasional use only.*

4 Mrs. T's frozen pierogies (any type)
    sautéed in
2 tsp regular margarine and
2 Tbsp chopped onions
3 oz bratwurst or kielbasa sausage (about a
    3-inch piece)
¾ cup steamed green beans
½ cup no-sugar-added applesauce

DINNER

1 Budget Gourmet Light Sirloin of Beef in
   Herb Sauce
½ cup cooked carrots
1 small corn muffin with
1 tsp margarine
2 pear halves with
¼ cup low-fat cottage cheese

2 slices Thin-n-Crispy Pizza Hut Pizza
   Supreme (⅓ of 10-inch pizza)
Tossed salad with
1 Tbsp dressing
½ cup fresh mixed fruit

DINNER

1 serving **Chicken Cacciatore**
⅔ cup cooked brown or white rice
Lettuce with one sliced orange and sliced
    red onion to taste
Dressing:
    2 tsp oil and
    2 tsp vinegar

Chicken Cacciatore

Yield: 4 servings / Serving size: 1¼ cups

INGREDIENTS

3-lb fryer chicken, cut up
Nonstick vegetable cooking spray
½ cup chopped onion
¼ cup chopped green pepper
½ cup chopped celery
1 28-oz can tomatoes
½ tsp salt
1 clove garlic, minced
1 tsp parsley flakes
Dash oregano
1 Tbsp cornstarch
¼ cup water

METHOD

1. Brown pieces of chicken in skillet sprayed with vegetable spray.
2. Add vegetables, salt, and spices. Cover and simmer 1 hour.
3. Mix cornstarch with water and add to skillet, stirring until gravy thickens.

1 serving **Shrimp Skewers**
⅔ cup cooked brown or white rice
½ cup sugar-free gelatin cubes with
2 Tbsp whipped topping

Shrimp Skewers

Yield: 1 serving (3 skewers)

INGREDIENTS

6 oz (about 9) large shrimp
3 cherry tomatoes
3 pearl onions
3 1-inch pieces green pepper
6 ½-inch slices zucchini
3 whole mushrooms
¾ cup unsweetened pineapple chunks
2 Tbsp Italian dressing

METHOD

1. Alternate shrimp, vegetables, and pineapple on 3 skewers.
2. Broil or grill about 5 minutes on each side or until done. Baste with Italian dressing while cooking. Serve over rice.

DINNER

1 **Chicken Taco**
⅓ cup refried beans
Fresh vegetable relish tray
1 serving **Pears Filled With Strawberry Cream Cheese** (page 105)

Chicken Tacos

Yield: 12 tacos / Serving size: 1 taco

INGREDIENTS
1 3- to 3½-lb chicken
1 pkg. taco seasoning mix
1½ cups water
12 6-inch flour tortillas
6 oz cheddar cheese, shredded
Shredded lettuce
Chopped tomato
Chopped onion

METHOD
1. Remove skin from chicken and simmer until meat falls off the bone. Cut meat into small pieces.
2. In a skillet, combine cooked chicken, taco seasoning, and water. Bring to a boil, then simmer to desired consistency (10–15 minutes).
3. Heat tortillas in microwave or iron skillet. Place 2 oz cooked chicken in the center of each tortilla. Top with ½ oz cheese, lettuce, tomato, and onion. Roll up.

DINNER

Pears Filled With Strawberry Cream Cheese

Yield: 2 servings / Serving size: ½ pear with 2 oz cream cheese

INGREDIENTS

4 oz low-fat cream cheese
2 fresh strawberries, sliced
¼ tsp brown sugar substitute
1 pear, unpeeled and halved
1 tsp lemon juice

METHOD

1. Combine cream cheese, strawberries, and brown sugar substitute in food processor or blender. Blend until smooth.
2. Spread each pear half with lemon juice, then top with half of the cream cheese mixture.

DINNER

1 serving **Kung Pao Chicken**
⅔ cup cooked rice
1 cup Chinese kale
1 cup melon balls

Kung Pao Chicken

Yield: 4 servings / Serving size: ¼ recipe

INGREDIENTS

12 oz boneless chicken, diced
1 tsp rice wine
1 egg white
1 Tbsp cornstarch
2 Tbsp vegetable oil
Nonstick vegetable cooking spray
1 Tbsp cooking wine
1 clove garlic, minced
1 green onion, chopped
2 red chili peppers, chopped
1 slice fresh ginger
1½ tsp salt
½ tsp sugar
Chinese hot sauce, if desired

METHOD

1. Season chicken with rice wine, egg white, cornstarch, and 1 Tbsp vegetable oil.
2. Spray wok with vegetable spray. Stir-fry chicken until done.
3. Remove chicken and clean wok. Spray again with vegetable spray. Add remaining 1 Tbsp vegetable oil. Heat oil and sauté garlic, onion, chili peppers, ginger, salt, sugar, and hot sauce. Add wine and chicken. Stir. Serve over rice.

9

2 slices **Nutty Rice Loaf**
Tossed salad with
2 Tbsp reduced-calorie dressing
1¼ cups watermelon cubes

Nutty Rice Loaf

Yield: 6 slices / Serving size: 1 slice

INGREDIENTS
Nonstick vegetable cooking spray
1½ cups cooked brown rice
1 cup shredded zucchini
¼ cup chopped onion
½ cup wheat germ
¼ cup chopped walnuts
1 cup shredded medium-sharp cheddar cheese
3 eggs, lightly beaten
½ tsp thyme
½ tsp marjoram
¼ tsp pepper

METHOD
1. Preheat oven to 350 degrees. Spray a 9- by 5-inch loaf pan with vegetable spray.
2. Combine all ingredients. Pack into loaf pan.
3. Bake for 40–45 minutes or until brown on edges and firm to the touch.
4. Cut into slices. Serve hot or at room temperature.

DINNER

1 Crab Cake
½ cup green peas
½ cup steamed carrots
1 Tbsp reduced-calorie margarine
1 3-inch slice French bread
Tossed salad with
2 Tbsp Parmesan cheese and
2 Tbsp reduced-calorie dressing
1 baked apple with
Dash cinnamon

Crab Cakes

Yield: 4 servings / Serving size: 1 crab cake

INGREDIENTS

Nonstick vegetable cooking
  spray
½ lb lump crab meat, flaked
1 Tbsp Dijon mustard
1 Tbsp margarine, melted
1 egg
1½ tsp lemon juice

½ tsp Worcestershire sauce
Pinch cayenne pepper
⅛ tsp salt
2 dashes Tabasco sauce
½ cup soft bread crumbs
Lemon wedges (optional)

METHOD

1. Preheat oven to 400 degrees. Spray cookie sheet with vegetable spray.
2. Combine crab meat, mustard, margarine, egg, lemon juice, Worcestershire sauce, and seasonings. Add 2–4 Tbsp bread crumbs to bind.
3. Shape into 4 cakes (½ cup mixture for each). Roll in remaining bread crumbs; place on cookie sheet.
4. Bake for 20–25 minutes or until lightly browned, turning crab cakes over halfway through cooking time. Serve with lemon wedges, if desired.

½ Greek Florentine Pizza
8 oz nonfat artificially sweetened lemon
  yogurt
1 granola bar

Greek Florentine Pizza

Yield: 2 servings / Serving size: ½ pizza

INGREDIENTS
½ tsp olive oil
1 cup frozen spinach, thawed and squeezed dry
1 clove garlic, minced
1 small pizza crust
¼ cup spaghetti sauce
¼ tsp Italian herbs
1 Tbsp sesame seeds
1 tomato, sliced
2 oz feta cheese

METHOD
1. Preheat oven to 425 degrees.
2. Heat nonstick skillet. Add oil, spinach, and garlic. Sauté until hot throughout. Remove from heat.
3. Spread sauce on crust. Sprinkle with herbs.
4. Arrange spinach in a circle on crust. Sprinkle with sesame seeds. Arrange sliced tomatoes in a circle. Crumble cheese on top. Bake 15 minutes.

DINNER

1 serving **Oven-Fried Fish**
½ cup corn
½ cup Italian green beans with pimento garnish and
1 tsp margarine
1 cup cabbage slaw with
Green pepper, diced,
Carrots, shredded, and
2 Tbsp reduced-calorie dressing
¼ cup orange sherbet

Oven-Fried Fish

Yield: 4 servings / Serving size: 3 oz

INGREDIENTS

1 lb fish fillets (cut into 4 pieces)
2 cups cornflakes
1 tsp salt
⅛ tsp pepper
¼ cup evaporated skim milk
4 tsp vegetable oil

METHOD

1. Preheat oven to 500 degrees.
2. Roll cornflakes into fine crumbs between layers of waxed paper. Add salt and pepper.
3. Pour milk into shallow pan. Dip fish in milk, then crumbs.
4. Arrange fish on baking sheet sprayed with vegetable spray. Sprinkle oil over fish.
5. Bake for 10 minutes.

2 Stuffed Zucchini halves
⅔ cup cooked brown rice
1 cup skim or 1% milk

Stuffed Zucchini

Yield: 4 servings / Serving size: 2 zucchini halves

INGREDIENTS

4 whole zucchini, about 7 inches long
6 Tbsp margarine or olive oil
1 medium onion, diced
1 large green pepper, diced
2 cups chopped mushrooms
1 10-oz pkg. frozen spinach, thawed
2 Tbsp pimento, diced
2 eggs

2 cups fat-free bread crumbs
2 tsp salt (optional)
¼ tsp garlic powder
¼ tsp onion powder
¼ tsp nutmeg (optional)
2 Tbsp thyme
6 oz Swiss cheese
1 30-oz jar herb and garlic tomato sauce

METHOD

1. Cut zucchini in half lengthwise and scoop out some of the inside to form a shell. Steam shell for 2–3 minutes, drain well, and cool.
2. Sauté onion, green pepper, and mushrooms in margarine until soft. Cool.
3. Drain thawed spinach of extra water. Mix spinach, onion, pepper, and mushrooms with pimento, eggs, bread crumbs, salt, garlic powder, onion powder, nutmeg, and thyme.
4. Fill zucchini shells with stuffing and place in a baking dish. Cover with tomato sauce and Swiss cheese.
5. Bake at 350 degrees for 15–20 minutes until cheese is melted and sauce bubbles.

DINNER

1 serving **Chicken-Fried Steak With Pan Gravy**
¾ cup mashed potatoes
1 cup green beans
Dinner roll with
2 tsp margarine
1 orange

Chicken-Fried Steak With Pan Gravy

Yield: 4 servings / Serving size: 1 piece with gravy

INGREDIENTS

1 lb round steak, pounded thin
1 egg, beaten with water
½ tsp salt
¼–½ tsp garlic powder
¼ tsp pepper
¼ cup flour for dredging
Nonstick vegetable cooking spray
1 Tbsp vegetable oil
1 Tbsp water
Gravy:
   2 Tbsp flour
   ½ cup water
   ½ cup skim or 1% milk

1. Cut away fat from steak, remove bone, and cut into 4 pieces.
2. Beat egg with water until lemon-colored.
3. Combine salt, garlic powder, and pepper. Sprinkle seasonings on both sides of steak.
4. Dredge in flour and shake off excess; dip in egg and again in flour.
5. Coat a large skillet with vegetable spray and heat it; add vegetable oil.
6. Brown both sides of meat, turning only once. Reduce heat to low. Cook for 10–15 minutes until juices run clear. Add 1 Tbsp water to skillet, cover, and cook for 5 minutes.
7. Remove steak to heated plate. Add flour to drippings; when light brown, stir in water and milk, whisking until it thickens into a gravy. Add more water if gravy is too thick.
8. Return steaks to skillet; simmer gently until ready to serve.

DINNER

3 oz broiled fish (haddock, halibut, or
   salmon) with
Lemon wedge
½ cup steamed green beans and onions
¾ cup baked acorn squash
1 whole-wheat dinner roll with
1 Tbsp reduced-calorie margarine
Tossed salad with
2 Tbsp reduced-calorie dressing
1 cup **Gelatin Fruit Parfait**

Gelatin Fruit Parfait

Yield: 1 serving

INGREDIENTS

½ cup sliced fresh fruit
½ cup sugar-free gelatin
2 Tbsp whipped topping
Dash nutmeg or cinnamon (optional)

METHOD

1. Prepare sugar-free gelatin according to package
   directions.
2. Alternate layers of fruit and gelatin in parfait glass.
3. Garnish with whipped topping and dash of nutmeg or
   cinnamon, if desired.

16

1 serving **Crustless Spinach Quiche**
2 3-inch slices French bread
1 cup cooked carrots with
2 tsp margarine
Tossed salad with
2 Tbsp reduced-calorie dressing
1 cup cantaloupe cubes

Crustless Spinach Quiche

Yield: 6 servings / Serving size: ⅙ pie

INGREDIENTS

1 10-oz pkg. frozen chopped spinach
8 oz part-skim mozzarella cheese, grated
4 eggs plus 2 egg whites lightly beaten or 1½ cups egg
   substitute
4 tsp grated onion
¼ tsp nutmeg
Salt (optional) and pepper to taste
Nonstick vegetable cooking spray

METHOD

1. Preheat oven to 350 degrees.
2. Place spinach in colander to thaw; press out all
    moisture.
3. Mix spinach with cheese, eggs, onion, nutmeg, salt, and
    pepper.
4. Transfer to an 8-inch pie plate coated with vegetable
    spray.
5. Bake 30 minutes or until knife inserted in center comes
    out clean. Serve hot or cold.

DINNER

1 baked medium pork chop or 2 small lamb
    chops
½ cup noodles
1 whole-wheat dinner roll with
2 tsp margarine
1 serving **Crisp Red Cabbage**
½ cup fresh fruit salad

Crisp Red Cabbage

Yield: 6 servings / Serving size: ½ cup

INGREDIENTS
4 cups (about ¾ lb) shredded red cabbage
2 apples, cored and cut into wedges
¼ cup red wine vinegar
2 Tbsp brown sugar
¼ tsp salt
¼ tsp nutmeg

METHOD
1. Place cabbage, apples, vinegar, and brown sugar in saucepan over medium heat. Mix well.
2. Cover and simmer about 10 minutes until cabbage is tender-crisp.
3. Add salt and nutmeg. Mix well. Serve warm.

1 serving **Sally's Hawaiian Chicken**
⅓ cup cooked brown or white rice
1 cup oriental mixed vegetables (frozen variety), stir-fried with
2 tsp olive oil
1 kiwifruit

Sally's Hawaiian Chicken

Yield: 8 servings
Serving size: ½ breast, or 1 wing and 1 thigh, or 1 thigh and 1 leg

INGREDIENTS

3 lb chicken, broiler or fryer, cut up
1½ tsp salt (optional)
1 20-oz can no-sugar-added chunk pineapple
1 cup sliced mushrooms
½ cup water
2 Tbsp soy sauce
2 tsp chicken bouillon
½ tsp ginger
½ green pepper, chopped

METHOD

1. Sprinkle salt on chicken parts and broil. Turn and brown other side.
2. Combine remaining ingredients, including pineapple juice, and pour over chicken.
3. Bake uncovered in 375-degree oven for 45 minutes or until chicken is browned.

DINNER

1 serving **Vegetarian Lasagna**
1 3-inch slice French bread with
1 tsp margarine
Tossed salad with
2 Tbsp reduced-calorie dressing
1 small nectarine

Vegetarian Lasagna

Yield: 6 servings / Serving size: 4½- by 4-inch piece

INGREDIENTS

6 lasagna noodles
2 qt water
2 Tbsp vegetable oil
1 cup chopped onion
1½ cups (about 4 medium) ⅛-inch bias-cut carrots
2 tsp minced garlic
1¾ cups spaghetti sauce (about 1 15-oz jar)
½ cup water
1 tsp basil
½ tsp oregano
2 eggs
2 cups low-fat cottage cheese
4 Tbsp Parmesan cheese
1 10-oz pkg. frozen chopped spinach, thawed and drained
1 cup sliced mushrooms
1 cup quartered and sliced zucchini
¼ cup sliced black olives (optional)
1 cup shredded part-skim mozzarella cheese

METHOD

1. Cook lasagna noodles in boiling water about 12 minutes. Drain, rinse, and cover with cold water.
2. Heat vegetable oil in saucepan. Add onion, carrots, and garlic. Sauté until carrots are tender, about 10 minutes.
3. Add spaghetti sauce, water, and spices. Bring to a simmer.
4. Beat eggs and blend in cottage cheese, Parmesan cheese, and vegetables.
5. Spread a thin layer of sauce over bottom of 9- by 13-inch baking pan. Cover with a layer of noodles. Spoon half of cheese-vegetable mixture over noodles. Cover with half of sauce. Repeat.
6. Cover with foil and bake at 350 degrees for 35 minutes.
7. Remove foil. Arrange olive slices over top and sprinkle with mozzarella cheese. Bake uncovered about 15 minutes, or until center is bubbly.
8. Let stand about 10 minutes to set layers. Cut into 6 pieces.

DINNER

½ breast **Oven-Fried Chicken**
1 cup mashed potatoes (made with skim or
    1% milk) with
2 Tbsp prepared gravy
1 cup steamed green beans
1 **Baked Apple I** (page 121)

Oven-Fried Chicken

Yield: 2 servings / Serving size: ½ breast

INGREDIENTS

1 whole chicken breast
6 saltine crackers, crushed
2 tsp Parmesan cheese
¼ tsp pepper
⅛ tsp each: basil, celery seed, onion powder, oregano,
    paprika, and salt
1½ Tbsp evaporated skim milk
1 Tbsp vegetable oil

METHOD

1. Combine cracker crumbs, cheese, pepper, basil, celery
   seed, onion powder, oregano, paprika, and salt in bowl.
2. Dip chicken in evaporated milk and then coat with
   crumb mixture. Place in lightly greased shallow roasting
   pan.
3. Bake in 400-degree oven for 30 minutes. Brush with oil
   and bake 10 minutes longer.

Baked Apple I

Yield: 1 serving

INGREDIENTS

1 apple, cored
½ can sugar-free lemon-lime soda
Cinnamon

METHOD

1. Core apple. Sprinkle with cinnamon and pour soda over apple.
2. Bake in 350-degree oven for 20–30 minutes.

DINNER

1 serving **Meat Loaf**
1 medium baked potato with
2 Tbsp sour cream
1 cup steamed Brussels sprouts
1 cup coleslaw made with
2 Tbsp reduced-calorie dressing

Meat Loaf

Yield: 6 servings / Serving size: 1½-inch slice

INGREDIENTS
1½ lb ground beef
1 cup fine bread crumbs
2 eggs
1 8-oz can tomato sauce
½ cup chopped onion
2 Tbsp chopped green pepper
1½ tsp salt
1 medium bay leaf, crushed
Dash thyme
Dash marjoram

METHOD
1. Preheat oven to 350 degrees.
2. Combine all ingredients; mix well.
3. Pat into 9-inch loaf pan.
4. Bake for 1 hour.

Note: half of recipe yields a 3-serving loaf; one-third of recipe yields a 2-serving loaf.

1 serving **Grilled Pork Loin**
2 small new potatoes, boiled
1 3-inch slice French bread with
1 tsp margarine
Tossed green salad with
2 Tbsp reduced-calorie dressing
¾ cup fresh pineapple

Grilled Pork Loin

Yield: 4 servings / Serving size: ¼ recipe

INGREDIENTS

1 lb boneless center-cut pork loin, trimmed of excess fat
4 tomatoes
3 Tbsp minced fresh basil

METHOD

1. Cut pork loin into 4 equal cutlets no more than ½ inch thick.
2. Slice tomatoes about ¼–½ inch thick and set aside. Mince basil and set aside.
3. Grill pork loin on barbecue grill. When first side is done, turn pork over and place basil and sliced tomatoes on top. Cover grill if possible and continue cooking until pork is done. If you cannot cover the grill, cutlets can be placed in a microwave after grilling to cook the tomatoes slightly.

DINNER

1 serving **Orange Roughy Picante**
1 cup cooked Spanish rice
½ cup green beans
1 slice whole-wheat bread
1¼ cups watermelon, cubed

Orange Roughy Picante

Yield: 4 servings / Serving size: 4 oz

INGREDIENTS

16 oz orange roughy fillet
½ 16-oz jar mild picante sauce
¼ cup chopped onion
¼ cup chopped green pepper
¼ cup sliced mushrooms
¼ cup grated cheddar cheese

METHOD

1. Place fish in microwave-safe dish. Cover with picante sauce, and sprinkle with onion, green pepper, and mushrooms. Cover with cheese.
2. Place plastic wrap over dish and vent. Microwave on high for 4 minutes or until fish flakes easily with fork. Divide fish into 4 equal portions. To prepare in conventional oven, bake at 400 degrees for 15 minutes.

DINNER

1 serving **Sausage and Corn Bread Pie**
½ cup steamed green beans
Tossed salad with
2 Tbsp reduced-calorie dressing
1 medium pear

Sausage and Corn Bread Pie

Yield: 4 servings / Serving size: ¼ recipe

INGREDIENTS

14 oz turkey sausage
1 cup chopped onion
1 clove garlic, crushed
1 28-oz can tomatoes
  (reserve juice)
¼ cup green chilies,
  chopped and undrained
¾ cup frozen corn
1 tsp chili powder
Nonstick vegetable cooking
  spray

⅔ cup cornmeal
¼ cup whole-wheat or
  white flour
1½ tsp baking powder
¼ tsp salt
1 egg, beaten
⅓ cup skim or 1% milk
1 Tbsp corn oil

METHOD

1. Cook sausage, onion, and garlic in a large skillet over medium heat until meat is browned and crumbled.
2. Add tomatoes, juice, chilies, corn, and chili powder and simmer 20 minutes. Spoon mixture into an 8-inch baking dish that has been coated with vegetable spray. Set aside.
3. Combine cornmeal, flour, baking powder, and salt in a medium bowl, mixing well.
4. Combine egg, milk, and oil in a small bowl. Add to dry ingredients, stirring just until moistened.
5. Spread corn bread mixture over sausage mixture. Bake at 375 degrees for 30–40 minutes or until golden brown.

DINNER

1 serving **Spinach Manicotti**
1 small dinner roll with
1 tsp margarine
Tossed salad with
2 Tbsp part-skim mozzarella cheese
1 small pear

Spinach Manicotti

Yield: 5 servings / Serving size: 1/5 recipe

INGREDIENTS

10 manicotti shells
2 6-oz cans tomato paste
3 cups water
1/2 cup finely chopped onion
2 cloves garlic, crushed
1/2 tsp dried whole basil
1/2 tsp dried whole oregano
1/4 tsp salt (optional)
1/4 tsp pepper

2 10-oz pkgs. frozen
    chopped spinach
1 16-oz carton low-fat
    cottage cheese
1/3 cup Parmesan cheese
1/4 tsp ground nutmeg
Nonstick vegetable cooking
    spray
1 tsp chopped fresh parsley

METHOD

1. Cook manicotti shells according to package directions, omitting salt; drain and set aside.
2. Combine next 8 ingredients; cover and cook sauce over low heat for 1 hour.
3. Cook spinach according to package directions, omitting salt. Drain; place on paper towels and squeeze until barely moist. Combine spinach, cottage cheese, Parmesan cheese, and nutmeg. Stuff manicotti shells with spinach mixture and arrange in a 13- by 9- by 2-inch baking dish coated with vegetable spray.
4. Pour tomato sauce over manicotti. Bake at 350 degrees for 45 minutes. Garnish with parsley.

1 serving **Chicken Fajita**
⅓ cup corn
1 medium orange

Chicken Fajita

Yield: 4 servings
Serving size: ½ cup meat plus onions, peppers, and tortilla

INGREDIENTS

1 clove garlic, minced
2 tsp vegetable oil
2½ tsp lemon juice
1½ Tbsp soy sauce
Dash pepper
2 tsp Mexican seasoning
2 whole skinless chicken breasts, split
⅔ onion, thinly sliced
1 green pepper, thinly sliced
4 flour tortillas

METHOD

1. Make marinade by combining garlic, oil, lemon juice, soy sauce, pepper, and Mexican seasoning.
2. Cut chicken into thin strips. Add chicken to marinade, toss to coat evenly, and marinate in refrigerator for at least 2 hours. Stir mixture occasionally to recoat meat.
3. In a nonstick skillet, heat 1 tsp oil on medium-high heat. Add onions and peppers. Sauté, stirring occasionally, until onion is slightly brown but still crisp and tender.
4. Cook chicken with only 1 tsp oil in another nonstick skillet on medium-high heat until no longer pink. Serve with onions and green peppers on tortilla.

1 serving **Grilled Tuna Steak**
1 cup steamed new potatoes
Fresh spinach salad with
2 Tbsp reduced-calorie dressing
1 kiwifruit

Grilled Tuna Steak

Yield: 6 servings / Serving size: 4 oz (5 oz before cooking)

INGREDIENTS

2 lb yellowfin tuna steaks, fresh or frozen
½ cup vegetable oil
¼ cup lemon juice
2 tsp salt
½ tsp Worcestershire sauce
¼ tsp white pepper
⅛ tsp hot pepper sauce
Paprika

METHOD

1. Cut into 6 equal portions and place on grill.
2. Combine remaining ingredients, except paprika. Baste fish with sauce and sprinkle with paprika.
3. Cook about 4 inches from moderately hot coals for 5–6 minutes. Turn, baste with sauce, and sprinkle with paprika; cook 4–5 minutes longer or until tuna has a slightly pink center.

1 serving **Turkey Polynesian**
⅔ cup cooked brown or white rice
Tossed salad with
2 Tbsp reduced-calorie dressing
½ cup sugar-free gelatin with
2 Tbsp whipped topping

Turkey Polynesian

Yield: 4 servings / Serving size: ¼ recipe

INGREDIENTS

2 tsp cornstarch
1½ tsp water
¾ tsp soy sauce
¾ tsp salt (optional)
12 oz uncooked turkey
  breast, skinned, boned,
  and cubed
½ cup sliced onions
1 Tbsp vegetable oil

⅔ cup sliced celery
4 oz water chestnuts,
  drained and sliced
⅔ cup snow peas
⅔ cup undrained no-sugar-
  added pineapple chunks
  (reserve ⅔ cup juice)
⅓ cup mandarin oranges,
  drained

METHOD

1. In small bowl, combine cornstarch, water, soy sauce, and salt. Mix well. Coat turkey cubes with cornstarch mixture.
2. In nonstick skillet over medium heat, sauté onions in half the oil.
3. Add celery, water chestnuts, and snow peas. Cook for 2 minutes. Remove vegetables from skillet.
4. To skillet, add remaining oil and turkey. Sauté until brown. Add sautéed vegetables, pineapple, and juice. Simmer for 10 minutes. Remove from heat. Add oranges. Serve over hot rice.

DINNER

3 oz roasted beef brisket
1 serving **Noodle Pudding**
½ cup sorrel or cooked carrots with
1 tsp margarine
1 cup mixed fruit salad

Noodle Pudding

Yield: 4 servings / Serving size: ½ cup

INGREDIENTS

1 egg
½ Tbsp sugar
Dash nutmeg
⅛ tsp cinnamon
1¼ cups broad noodles, cooked
½ Tbsp vegetable oil
½ cup apple juice
¼ cup raisins
1 Tbsp chopped pecans

METHOD

1. Beat egg and sugar until fluffy. Add remaining ingredients, except nuts.
2. Pour into well-greased 8-inch baking pan. Sprinkle in nuts.
3. Bake in 350-degree oven for 40 minutes or until browned.

1 serving **Grilled Lobster Tails**
1 baked potato with
2 Tbsp low-fat sour cream
1 cup steamed broccoli
⅓ cup frozen yogurt
1 cup fresh or no-sugar-added frozen
   strawberries

Grilled Lobster Tails

Yield: 4 servings / Serving size: 3 oz

INGREDIENTS

2 6-oz lobster tails (or 12 oz frozen shelled lobster meat)
2 Tbsp butter
¼ cup white wine
¼ tsp lemon pepper or your favorite seasoning

METHOD

1. Melt butter and combine with wine (much of the
   alcohol will evaporate, leaving only the flavor) and
   seasoning.
2. Cut down the back of the lobster tails and gently spread
   apart. Baste with sauce. Place on a hot grill and
   continue to baste frequently. Cook for 8 minutes. Baste
   and turn. Cook for 5 more minutes or until done.

DINNER

1 serving **Chicken With Sun-Dried Tomatoes**
⅔ cup cooked brown or white rice
Tossed salad with
2 Tbsp reduced-calorie dressing
1 medium peach

Chicken With Sun-Dried Tomatoes

Yield: 4 servings / Serving size: ¼ recipe

INGREDIENTS

4 skinless, boneless chicken breast halves (about 1 lb total),
 trimmed of cartilage and fat
1 Tbsp reduced-calorie margarine
¼ tsp freshly ground pepper
1 large shallot, minced
⅔ cup chicken broth
½ cup dry white wine
⅛ tsp marjoram
¼ cup chopped sun-dried tomatoes

METHOD

1. Cut each chicken breast half into 6 equal parts. Using a nonstick skillet, melt the margarine over high heat. When the foam begins to subside, add chicken pieces.
2. Sprinkle with pepper. Sauté over moderate heat, turning, until the chicken is just opaque throughout, 4–5 minutes.
3. Remove chicken with a slotted spoon. Add shallot to the skillet and sauté, stirring until softened, about 1 minute. Add broth, wine (much of the alcohol will evaporate, leaving only the flavor), marjoram, and tomatoes.
4. Bring to a boil over moderate heat and cook, uncovered, for 5 minutes, stirring occasionally.
5. Return the chicken to the skillet. Simmer, gently spooning the sauce over the chicken, until heated through. Simmer until the sauce is reduced by half.

DINNER

1 serving **Corn Soufflé**
1 small whole-wheat dinner roll with
1 tsp margarine
½ cup steamed carrots
1 cup steamed green beans

Corn Soufflé

Yield: 2 servings / Serving size: ½ recipe

INGREDIENTS

2 tsp margarine
2 Tbsp flour
1 cup skim or 1% milk
Salt and pepper to taste
¼ tsp garlic powder
3 eggs, separated
2 cups canned corn, drained
Nonstick vegetable cooking spray

METHOD

1. Melt margarine in medium saucepan over low heat. Add flour and stir until smooth. Cook 1 minute, stirring constantly. Gradually add milk and cook over medium heat, stirring constantly, until thick and bubbly. Stir in salt, pepper, and garlic powder.
2. Beat egg yolks until thick. Gradually stir about one-quarter of white sauce into yolks. Add remaining sauce and stir in corn.
3. Beat egg whites until stiff. Gently fold into corn mixture. Spoon mixture into a small 1½-qt soufflé dish that has been coated with vegetable spray.
4. Bake at 350 degrees for 50 minutes or until puffed and golden. Serve immediately.

DINNER

1 serving **Herbed Pork Kabobs**
⅔ cup cooked brown and wild rice mixture
1 cup sliced tomato sprinkled with basil and
  rice wine vinegar
½ mango

Herbed Pork Kabobs

Yield: 4 servings / Serving size: 4-oz skewer

INGREDIENTS

1 lb pork tenderloin
¼ cup dry white wine
¾ tsp dried marjoram
¾ tsp dried rosemary
1 garlic clove, minced
3 Tbsp margarine, softened
¼ tsp salt (optional)
Pinch pepper

METHOD

1. Combine trimmed pork, wine (much of the alcohol will evaporate, leaving only the flavor), ¼ tsp marjoram, ¼ tsp rosemary, and garlic in medium bowl; toss to coat. Let stand at room temperature for 20 minutes.
2. Cream together margarine, ½ tsp marjoram, ½ tsp rosemary, salt, and pepper.
3. Drain pork; reserve marinade. Beat marinade into margarine mix.
4. Cut pork into 1½-inch cubes and thread on 4 skewers.
5. Place on a wire rack over a shallow baking dish. Broil 4 inches from heat, turning frequently and basting occasionally with herb-butter mix. Brown meat on all sides. Serve with lemon wedges.

DINNER

1 serving **Hearty Bean Stew** topped with 1½ oz grated part-skim mozzarella cheese
Tossed salad with
2 Tbsp reduced-calorie dressing
½ cup reduced-calorie cranberry juice cocktail

Hearty Bean Stew

Yield: 4 servings / Serving size: 1 cup

INGREDIENTS

1 15½-oz can kidney beans, undrained
½ 15-oz can garbanzo beans, undrained
1¼ cups water
1 medium potato, peeled, quartered lengthwise, and diced
½ cup thinly sliced carrots
¼ cup chopped onions
½ 6-oz can tomato paste
1 tsp chili powder
½ tsp salt (optional)
½ tsp crushed dried basil
⅛ tsp garlic powder

METHOD

1. In a Dutch oven, combine all ingredients. Bring to boil; reduce heat. Cover and simmer 30 minutes or until vegetables are tender.

1 serving **Pork Dijon**
⅔ cup cooked brown rice
1 cup steamed French-cut green beans with
1 tsp margarine
1¼ cups strawberries with
2 Tbsp low-fat sour cream

Pork Dijon

Yield: 4 servings / Serving size: ¼ recipe

INGREDIENTS
1 lb pork tenderloin
2 tsp olive oil
1 cup chicken broth
2 Tbsp Dijon mustard
1 Tbsp cornstarch

METHOD
1. Cut tenderloin into medallions. Sauté medallions in hot oil in a nonstick frying pan until brown.
2. Mix together chicken broth, mustard, and cornstarch. Pour over medallions.
3. Cook, stirring sauce until thickened; cover and simmer until pork is done. Divide into 4 equal portions.

DINNER

1 serving **Chicken-Okra Gumbo**
½ cup cooked broccoli with
1 tsp margarine
2 halves no-sugar-added canned pears

Chicken-Okra Gumbo

Yield: 4 servings / Serving size: ½ chicken breast

INGREDIENTS

2 whole skinless chicken breasts, split
½ cup flour, divided
Salt to taste (optional)
Pepper to taste
1½ Tbsp reduced-calorie margarine
1 lb fresh okra, chopped
1 fresh tomato, chopped
1 medium onion, chopped
2 qt water

METHOD

1. Dredge chicken with mixture of ¼ cup flour, salt, and pepper. In a heavy skillet, fry chicken in margarine until brown. Set aside.
2. Fry okra, tomato, and onion in the same pan with the margarine used to cook the chicken. Set vegetables aside. Reserve 2 Tbsp fat from the pan.
3. In a 6-qt kettle, make a roux by adding ¼ cup flour to the reserved cooking fat, stirring constantly over low heat until it is light brown but not burnt.
4. Add water, salt, pepper, and vegetables. Stir for a few minutes. Add fried chicken. Cook for about 1 hour or until chicken is tender.

1 serving **Tamale Pie**
Tossed salad with
1 Tbsp reduced-calorie dressing
1 medium apple

37

Tamale Pie

Yield: 4 servings
Serving size: 1 cup meat mixture and ¼ cup topping

INGREDIENTS

¾ lb lean ground beef
¼ cup chopped green
  pepper
¼ cup chopped onion
1 tsp vegetable oil
½ tsp Mexican seasoning
1 cup canned tomatoes
  (reserve 1½ Tbsp juice)

¾ cup frozen corn
4 Tbsp green chilies
Nonstick vegetable cooking
  spray
1 pkg. corn bread mix
Paprika

METHOD

1. Sauté meat, peppers, onions, and seasoning together in oil.
2. Drain tomatoes and reserve liquid. Chop tomatoes and add to meat mixture. Add remaining filling ingredients, except corn bread mix and paprika, and simmer until well heated and flavors blend. Stir occasionally.
3. Place filling mixture in an 8-inch-square baking pan coated with vegetable spray. Preheat oven to 375 degrees.
4. Prepare corn bread mix according to package instructions. Divide 1 cup of corn bread batter into 4 equal portions. Spoon batter portions about 2 inches apart over the warm meat mixture.
5. Bake in preheated oven at 375 degrees for 30–40 minutes or until corn bread is done. Sprinkle top with paprika, and serve.

DINNER

1 serving **Bay Scallops Parmesan**
1 small baked potato with
2 Tbsp low-fat sour cream
½ cup steamed zucchini
1 slice **Chocolate Angel Food Cake** (page 141)
1 cup strawberries, fresh or frozen, unsweetened

Bay Scallops Parmesan

Yield: 4 servings / Serving size: ¼ recipe

INGREDIENTS

1½ lb bay scallops (shrimp or lobster chunks may be substituted)
2 Tbsp margarine
1 clove garlic, chopped
1 Tbsp white wine
2–4 Tbsp lemon juice (to taste)
⅓ cup Parmesan cheese

METHOD

1. Place margarine in microwave-safe dish and melt. Add garlic, wine (much of the alcohol will evaporate, leaving only the flavor), lemon, and scallops. Microwave on high for 4 minutes, stirring once after 2 minutes.
2. Place scallops on an individual serving dish that is oven-proof. Sprinkle with Parmesan cheese, and place under broiler until cheese is browned.

Chocolate Angel Food Cake

Yield: 32 ½-inch slices / Serving size: 1 slice

INGREDIENTS

1 14½-oz angel food cake mix
¼ cup sifted unsweetened cocoa
¼ tsp chocolate flavoring
1 Tbsp sifted powdered sugar

METHOD

1. Combine flour packet from cake mix with cocoa.
   Prepare cake according to package directions.
2. Fold chocolate flavoring into batter. Bake cake according
   to package directions.
3. Sprinkle cooled cake with powdered sugar.

DINNER

1 serving **Frogmore Stew**
Tossed salad with
2 Tbsp reduced-calorie French dressing
⅓ cup nonfat artificially sweetened frozen
   yogurt

Frogmore Stew

Yield: 8 servings / Serving size: ⅛ recipe

INGREDIENTS

1 Tbsp shrimp boil or other seafood seasonings
8 small-to-medium new potatoes
16 oz turkey kielbasa sausage, cut in ½-inch slices
8 5-inch corn cobettes
1 lb fresh shrimp shelled and deveined

METHOD

1. In a large pot, place 1 inch of water and seasonings.
   Bring to a boil.
2. Add potatoes and sausage; cook 15 minutes.
3. Add corn; cook 10 minutes.
4. Add shrimp; cook 10 minutes.

DINNER

40

1 serving **Mike's Veal**
1 cup cooked pasta (angel hair or
    vermicelli)
Tossed salad with
2 Tbsp reduced-calorie vinaigrette dressing
¾ cup mixed melon pieces, orange
    segments, and banana slices

Mike's Veal

Yield: 4 servings / Serving size: ¼ recipe

INGREDIENTS
1 lb veal for scallopini
¼ cup whole-wheat flour
2 cloves garlic, finely chopped
1 Tbsp olive oil or nonstick vegetable cooking spray
8 oz sliced mushrooms
½ cup wine (red or white)
2 tomatoes, diced

METHOD
1. Pound veal to tenderize, and divide into 4 pieces. Dust
    lightly with flour. Sauté garlic in saucepan containing
    olive oil or coated with vegetable spray, then lightly
    brown veal.
2. Remove veal and sauté mushrooms for a few minutes.
3. Add wine, veal, and tomatoes.
4. Cover and heat 2 minutes, then serve.

DINNER

1 serving **Vegetable Stir-Fry**
1 serving **Light and Creamy Yogurt Pie**
(page 145) with
2 Tbsp Raspberry Sauce

Blend 1 cup raspberries with 2 Tbsp orange juice and 2 pkgs. artificial sweetener.

Vegetable Stir-Fry

Yield: 4 servings / Serving size: ¼ recipe

INGREDIENTS
2 Tbsp olive oil
1 small onion, quartered
1 red pepper, thinly sliced
½ Tbsp grated fresh ginger
1 cup broccoli florets
1 lb tofu, drained and cubed
1 cup cooked cold spaghetti
8 oz Parmesan cheese

METHOD
1. Heat nonstick skillet or wok to medium high. Add oil and onion and stir 2 minutes.
2. Add pepper and stir 1 minute more.
3. Add ginger, broccoli, and tofu and stir 2 minutes more.
4. Add spaghetti and stir until mixture is thoroughly heated.
5. Top each serving with 2 oz Parmesan cheese.

Light and Creamy Yogurt Pie

Yield: 8 slices / Serving size: ⅛ recipe

INGREDIENTS

1 cup low-fat whipped topping
1 cup nonfat artificially sweetened yogurt
2 cups sliced strawberries or 1½ cups other fruit
1 store-bought graham cracker crust

METHOD

1. Fold yogurt into whipped topping and add most of the fruit.
2. Fill crust. Garnish with remaining fruit.
3. Chill or freeze. May be served frozen.

DINNER

1 serving **New England Chicken Croquettes**
⅓ cup cooked brown rice
½ cup cooked spinach with
1 tsp margarine
1 cup fresh raspberries

New England Chicken Croquettes

Yield: 8 croquettes / Serving size: 2 croquettes

INGREDIENTS

2 Tbsp margarine
2 Tbsp flour
1 cup skim or 1% milk
1 tsp Worcestershire sauce
½ tsp chervil
½ tsp salt
⅛ tsp white pepper
2 cups finely chopped cooked chicken
⅔ cup bread crumbs
2 eggs, lightly beaten
Nonstick vegetable cooking spray

METHOD

1. Preheat oven to 375 degrees.
2. Melt margarine over low heat; stir in flour until smooth. Add milk gradually, whisking until smooth; add Worcestershire sauce, chervil, salt, pepper, and chicken. Cool.
3. When cold, form into 8 balls using ⅓ cup mixture per ball.
4. Roll in bread crumbs, egg, and again in bread crumbs.
5. Place on cookie sheet well coated with vegetable spray. Bake for 25–30 minutes or until light golden brown.

1 serving **French Onion Soup**
1 oz French bread
2 oz lean roast beef
⅓ cantaloupe

French Onion Soup

Yield: 6 servings / Serving size: 1 cup

INGREDIENTS

5 cups thinly sliced onion
2 Tbsp butter or margarine
3 10½-oz cans condensed beef broth
1 qt water
½ tsp salt (optional)
Freshly ground pepper, to taste
6 slices French bread, toasted
½ cup grated Swiss cheese
2 Tbsp Parmesan cheese

METHOD

1. Sauté onions slowly in butter until they turn a delicate gold.
2. Add beef broth and water. Cover and simmer gently for 45 minutes. Add salt and pepper.
3. Place in large oven-proof soup tureen or individual bowls. Top with toasted French bread and sprinkle with grated Swiss and Parmesan cheese.
4. Bake at 400 degrees for 8 minutes.

DINNER

1 cup **Hoppin' John**
1 cup **Seasoned Greens** (page 149)
1 piece corn bread (2 by 2 by 1½ inches)
2 tangerines

Hoppin' John

Yield: 8 servings / Serving size: 1 cup

INGREDIENTS

1 cup raw cow peas (dried field peas) or dried black-eyed
  peas
4 cups water
1 cup uncooked brown rice
4 slices bacon, fried crisp and fat drained
1 medium onion, chopped

METHOD

1. Boil peas in lightly salted water until tender. Drain peas,
    reserving 1 cup liquid.
2. Add peas and pea liquid to rice, bacon, and onion.
3. Put in rice steamer or double boiler and cook for 1 hour
    or until rice is done.

DINNER

Seasoned Greens

Yield: 8 servings / Serving size: ½ cup

INGREDIENTS

1 large bunch collard, mustard, or turnip greens or 1 lb
   frozen greens
2 fresh center-cut pork chops, fat trimmed and chopped
Salt, pepper, and hot sauce to taste

METHOD

1. Rinse greens well in water. Cut or tear into small pieces.
   Peel and cut turnips, if included.
2. Place greens and pork in a 2-qt saucepan and cover with
   water. Bring to a boil and cook about 5 minutes.

DINNER

1 slice **Salmon Loaf**
1 cup steamed broccoli
1 small baked potato with
2 Tbsp sour cream and
1 tsp margarine
1¼ cups strawberries

Salmon Loaf

Yield: 4 servings / Serving size: 1 slice

Note: Not recommended for low-sodium diets.

INGREDIENTS

Nonstick vegetable cooking spray
1 15½-oz can salmon, undrained
2 eggs, beaten
2 cups soft bread cubes or ⅓ cup bread crumbs
2 Tbsp fresh chopped parsley
⅛ tsp pepper
1 small onion, chopped
2 Tbsp lemon juice

METHOD

1. Preheat oven to 350 degrees. Generously spray an 8½-by 2½-inch loaf pan with vegetable spray.
2. In a large bowl, flake salmon, removing bones and skin.
3. Add all remaining ingredients and mix well.
4. Press into loaf pan. Bake for 50–60 minutes or until golden brown and toothpick comes out clean.
5. Let stand 5 minutes. Loosen edges and lift out of pan onto serving platter. Cut into 4 slices.

1 serving **Picante Tofu and Rice**
Iced Cafe Mocha (page 192)
4 oz nonfat artificially sweetened fruit-
    flavored yogurt

Picante Tofu and Rice

Yield: 1 serving

INGREDIENTS
½ cup chopped red onion
½ cup each chopped green and red peppers
2 Tbsp chopped green chili peppers
1 clove garlic, minced
4 oz firm tofu, drained and cubed
1 tsp olive oil
⅓ cup uncooked rice
⅔ cup vegetable broth
⅓ cup picante sauce or salsa
⅛ tsp cumin and paprika
¼ tsp chili powder
Tomato wedges
⅛ avocado
1 oz low-fat Monterey Jack cheese (optional)

METHOD
1. Sauté onion, peppers, garlic, and tofu in oil until just tender-crisp.
2. Add rice, broth, and salsa. Bring to a boil. Reduce heat, cover and simmer 15 minutes until rice is tender.
3. Add seasonings. Toss and let stand until liquid is absorbed. Garnish with tomato, avocado, and cheese.

DINNER

1 cup **Broccoli-Corn Chowder**
1 oz cheddar cheese, sprinkled on soup
1 piece sourdough bread with
1 tsp regular margarine
Tossed salad with
2–3 Tbsp nonfat dressing
1 scoop nonfat artificially sweetened frozen
   yogurt (70 calories/serving)

Broccoli-Corn Chowder

Yield: 16 servings / Serving size: 1 cup

INGREDIENTS

1 qt no-salt-added chicken broth
1 10-oz pkg. frozen chopped broccoli
1 lb frozen whole-kernel corn
1½ cups sliced mushrooms or canned salt-free equivalent
1½ cups chopped onion
¼ cup unsalted margarine
¾ cup flour
½ tsp white pepper
2½ cups skim or 1% milk
¼ cup chopped pimentos

METHOD

1. In a large kettle, combine chicken broth, broccoli, and corn.
2. Bring to a boil. Reduce heat to low and simmer 15 minutes. Set aside.
3. Sauté mushrooms and onion in margarine.
4. Blend flour and pepper into mushroom mixture. Add to broccoli mixture.
5. Add milk and simmer on low heat for about 30 minutes, stirring occasionally.
6. Stir in pimentos before serving.

1 serving **Saucy Seafood Stir-Fry**
⅔ cup cooked brown rice
½ cup Waldorf Salad

Saucy Seafood Stir-Fry

Yield: 4 servings / Serving size: ¼ recipe

INGREDIENTS

1 cup broccoli florets
1 cup cauliflower florets
½ cup julienned carrots
¼ cup sliced red peppers
¼ cup sliced green peppers
¼ cup sliced yellow peppers
½ lb shrimp, peeled and
deveined

½ lb scallops
1 Tbsp low-fat mayonnaise
1 Tbsp reduced-calorie
margarine
Juice of 1 lemon
Nonstick vegetable cooking
spray

METHOD

1. Spray a large frying pan or wok with vegetable spray; heat to medium-high.
2. Stir-fry broccoli, cauliflower, and carrots about 4 minutes. Sprinkle with water if they start to burn. Then add peppers.
3. Add shrimp to mixture and continue heating until shrimp turn pink. Add scallops and continue heating until scallops turn white. Set aside.
4. Melt margarine in microwave or oven. Whip mayonnaise and melted margarine together until smooth. Add lemon juice.
5. Combine with stir-fry mixture. Toss to coat.

DINNER

1 cup cooked linguine
1 cup **Clam Sauce**
Fresh spinach salad:
  Spinach greens with
  Red onion rings,
  ½ cup water-packed mandarin orange
    sections, drained, and
  2 Tbsp reduced-calorie Catalina dressing

Clam Sauce

Yield: 5 cups / Serving size: 1 cup

Note: Clam sauce is high in sodium and is for occasional use only.

INGREDIENTS

2 tsp olive oil
1 cup chopped onion
2 cloves garlic, minced or pressed
½ green pepper, chopped
1½ cups sliced mushrooms
3 10-oz cans whole baby clams with liquid

1½ cups tomatoes, peeled, seeded, and diced
¼ cup low-fat whipping cream
Pepper to taste
¾ cup Parmesan cheese

METHOD

1. Heat skillet and add olive oil. Sauté onion, garlic, pepper, and mushrooms.
2. Add clams and liquid. Simmer to reduce liquid by one-third to one-half.
3. Add tomato and cream and simmer until large glossy bubbles form.
4. Season and toss with Parmesan cheese. Serve 1 cup of recipe over 1 cup of cooked linguine.

154

1 serving **Chicken Curry**
⅔ cup cooked rice with
1 tsp margarine and parsley
Tossed salad with
2 Tbsp reduced-calorie dressing
⅓ cup canned unsweetened pineapple
cubes

Chicken Curry

Yield: 6 servings / Serving size: ⅙ recipe

INGREDIENTS

2-inch piece fresh ginger,
peeled
12 cloves garlic
1 cup plus 2 Tbsp water
2 medium onions, sliced
1 Tbsp corn oil
2-inch piece cinnamon stick
6 whole cloves
3 big cardamom seeds
(optional)

2 tsp chili powder
1 tsp cumin seed
½ tsp salt (optional)
½ tsp turmeric powder
1 3-lb chicken, skinned and
cut into serving-size pieces
½ cup nonfat plain yogurt
2 tomatoes, peeled and
chopped
⅓ cup chopped cilantro

METHOD

1. Make a paste of the ginger, garlic, and 2 Tbsp water.
2. Sauté onion in corn oil until brown. Add all spices and
   chicken and yogurt; continue to cook, sprinkling with
   additional water as required to keep from sticking.
3. Cook until chicken browns (about 10 minutes). Add 1
   cup of water and let simmer on low heat for about 45
   minutes or until chicken is tender.
4. Add chopped tomato after about 30 minutes. Before
   serving, add cilantro.

DINNER

1 serving **Prune-Stuffed Tenderloin**
½ baked acorn squash with
1 tsp margarine
5 spears steamed asparagus
Tossed salad with
2 Tbsp reduced-calorie dressing

Prune-Stuffed Tenderloin

Yield: 4 servings / Serving size: ¼ recipe (2½-inch slice)

INGREDIENTS

15 dried pitted prunes, coarsely chopped
⅓ cup chicken broth
¼ cup chopped celery
¼ cup chopped onion
1 tsp vegetable oil
3 slices multigrain bread, cubed
⅛ tsp poultry seasoning
1 lb pork tenderloin
1 clove garlic, crushed
⅛ tsp fennel seeds
¼ tsp pepper
⅛ tsp salt
String
Nonstick vegetable cooking spray
1 Tbsp margarine

DINNER

METHOD

1. Bring prunes and broth to a boil in a saucepan. Remove from heat and let stand for 10 minutes.
2. Sauté celery and onion in oil until tender.
3. Place bread cubes and poultry seasoning in a large bowl. Toss to mix. Add celery, onions, prunes, and broth. Toss lightly to blend. Add more broth if dressing is too dry.
4. Preheat oven to 500 degrees. Trim excess fat from tenderloin. Cut lengthwise to within ½ inch of each end and almost to the bottom, leaving bottom connected. Open out the meat and pound sides of pocket to about ¼ inch thickness.
5. Combine garlic, fennel seeds, pepper, and salt and rub on the inside of the pocket.
6. Spoon stuffing into opening of tenderloin. Press gently to close. Tie tenderloin securely with heavy string at 1-inch intervals.
7. Place tenderloin on a roasting rack coated with vegetable spray. Place rack in roasting pan. Insert meat thermometer into thickest part of tenderloin.
8. Place tenderloin in oven and immediately reduce temperature to 350 degrees. Cook 20 minutes, then brush on melted margarine and cook an additional 10–15 minutes until meat thermometer reaches 170 degrees.
9. Remove from oven, cover with aluminum foil, and let stand 10 minutes before slicing into 4 equal portions.

DINNER

1 piece **Zucchini Lasagna**
1 cup steamed broccoli with
2 tsp margarine
1 cup skim or 1% milk
½ poached pear with
2 Tbsp Raspberry Sauce (page 144)

Zucchini Lasagna

Yield: 9 servings / Serving size: 5- by 3-inch piece

INGREDIENTS
Nonstick vegetable cooking spray
1 16-oz jar marinara sauce
1 8-oz can tomatoes
½ lb (9–12) lasagna noodles
15 oz ricotta cheese
2 eggs, beaten
¼ tsp dried basil
¼ tsp dried oregano
¼ cup Parmesan cheese
3 cups coarsely grated zucchini
⅛ tsp pepper
2 tsp flour
8 oz mozzarella, coarsely grated

METHOD

1. Preheat oven to 350 degrees. Coat a 9-inch-square baking dish with vegetable spray.
2. Combine marinara and tomatoes. Spread ½ cup of the mixture over bottom of dish. Arrange uncooked noodles in dish, breaking off ends to make them fit. Place ends in open spaces.
3. Combine ricotta, eggs, basil, oregano, and Parmesan. Spread over lasagna noodles. Top with more noodles and ½ cup more sauce.
4. Combine zucchini, pepper, and flour. Spoon into baking dish and spread to make a level layer. Top with more lasagna noodles and remaining sauce.
5. Cover dish with foil and place on a rimmed baking sheet. Bake 55–60 minutes or until noodles are tender. Remove foil and sprinkle with mozzarella. Bake 15–20 minutes more until cheese is golden brown (or place under broiler). After removing lasagna from oven, let stand 15 minutes before cutting.

DINNER

1½ cups **Brunswick Stew**
1 cup salad greens with
½ cup citrus sections and
Dressing:
    1 Tbsp orange juice
    1 Tbsp vinegar
    2 tsp vegetable oil

Brunswick Stew

Yield: 4 servings / Serving size: 1½ cups

INGREDIENTS

1 cup water
4 medium chicken thighs, skin and fat removed
2 celery stalks, chopped
½ cup chopped onion
1 28-oz can tomatoes and juice
1 Tbsp sugar
1 cup frozen lima beans
1 cup frozen corn
1 cup cubed potatoes
Salt and pepper to taste

METHOD

1. Combine first four ingredients in a medium saucepan and bring to a boil. Cover and simmer 1½–2 hours to make a broth.
2. Save the broth. Remove bones and chop chicken. Put chicken in the broth.
3. Add tomatoes, juice, sugar, lima beans, corn, and potatoes. Bring to a boil.
4. Cover, reduce heat, and simmer 30–40 minutes or until vegetables are tender.

1 serving **Chicken Ratatouille**
⅔ cup cooked barley
Tossed salad with
2 Tbsp reduced-calorie dressing
¾ cup mixed fresh fruit salad, topped with
2 Tbsp nonfat fruit-flavored yogurt

Chicken Ratatouille

Yield: 4 servings
Serving size: 1 breast half and 1½ cups vegetables

INGREDIENTS

4 chicken breast halves,
   boned, with skin removed
1 Tbsp olive oil
1 small eggplant, cubed
2 small zucchini, sliced
1 onion, sliced
½ lb mushrooms, sliced
1 green pepper, sliced

1 large tomato, cubed
½ tsp garlic powder
1 tsp dried parsley
1 tsp basil
1 tsp pepper
½ cup part-skim mozzarella
   cheese, grated

METHOD

1. Sauté chicken in olive oil about 2 minutes per side.
2. Add eggplant, zucchini, onion, mushrooms, and green
   pepper. Cook 10 minutes.
3. Add tomato and remaining ingredients, except cheese.
4. Simmer 3–5 minutes more.
5. Arrange chicken breasts on top of vegetables and
   sprinkle cheese over the breasts. Cook 1 more minute
   until cheese melts.
6. Serve over barley or rice.

1 serving **Yogurt Chicken Paprika**
½ cup cooked egg noodles
½ cup steamed spinach
1 serving **Old-Fashioned Banana Pudding**
(page 163)

Yogurt Chicken Paprika

Yield: 4 servings / Serving size: 1 breast plus ½ cup sauce

INGREDIENTS
1½ cups chopped onions
1 Tbsp butter
1 Tbsp paprika
4 chicken breast halves
1 cube chicken bouillon
1 Tbsp cornstarch
8 oz nonfat plain yogurt

METHOD
1. Sauté onion in butter in large skillet. Blend in paprika. Add chicken and brown well.
2. Dissolve bouillon in 1 cup hot water and add to skillet. Cover and simmer 30–40 minutes until chicken is tender.
3. Dissolve cornstarch in 1 Tbsp cold water. Blend into yogurt. Stir yogurt mixture into skillet and serve.

DINNER

Old-Fashioned Banana Pudding

Yield: 6 servings / Serving size: ⅓ cup

INGREDIENTS
1 1-oz pkg. sugar-free vanilla pudding
2 cups skim or 1% milk
12 vanilla wafers
2 large bananas

METHOD
1. Combine pudding mix and milk. Cook over medium heat, stirring frequently, until mixture boils, then remove from heat.
2. Place 2 cookies on bottom of each of 6 custard dishes. Alternate layers of bananas and pudding, starting and finishing with bananas.
3. Chill before serving.

DINNER

2 **Stuffed Vegetarian Peppers**
1 cup skim or 1% milk
½ cup **Italian Fruit Salad** (page 165)

Stuffed Vegetarian Peppers

Yield: 6 servings / Serving size: 2 peppers

INGREDIENTS

2 cups uncooked couscous
4 cups boiling water
6 red peppers
6 yellow peppers
¼ cup minced shallots
¼ cup plus 1 Tbsp olive oil

1 lb asparagus
3 Tbsp tarragon
2 cups peas
½ tsp pepper
½ tsp paprika

METHOD

1. Place couscous in a large bowl and cover with boiling water. Cover with plastic wrap and let sit for 20 minutes.
2. Slice tops off peppers and remove the white membranes and seeds. Steam peppers and their tops for 5–7 minutes until tender.
3. Sauté shallots in 1 Tbsp olive oil until translucent. Chop the tender parts of the asparagus into 1-inch pieces.
4. With a wooden spoon, fluff the couscous and add remaining ingredients, including ¼ cup olive oil. Mix thoroughly.
5. Stuff the mixture into the peppers, using about ⅔ cup per pepper. Cover with the tops of the peppers. Put the peppers into a large casserole dish with ¼ inch of water at the bottom. Cover and bake at 350 degrees in a preheated oven for 45 minutes.
6. To serve, discard each pepper top and sprinkle with paprika.

Italian Fruit Salad

Yield: 6 servings / Serving size: ½ cup

INGREDIENTS

¼ cup freshly squeezed orange juice
Juice and rind of ¼ lemon
1 apple, unpeeled, cubed
1 pear, unpeeled, cubed
¼ lb seedless grapes
1 peach (in season), peeled and sliced
1 banana, sliced
2 pkgs. artificial sweetener (optional)
1 Tbsp orange liqueur (optional)

METHOD

1. Combine orange juice and lemon rind and juice in a large bowl. As you cut fruit, mix it with juice to keep it from discoloring.
2. Add sweetener and orange liqueur to taste. Toss lightly.
3. Cover bowl with plastic wrap and chill at least 2 hours before serving.

DINNER

1 serving **Oriental Chicken**
⅓ cup cooked rice or oriental noodles
Tossed salad with
1 tsp oil and
Vinegar to taste
¾ cup **Fruit Crisp** (page 167)
1 cup skim or 1% milk

Oriental Chicken

Yield: 4 servings / Serving size: ¼ recipe

INGREDIENTS

4 chicken thighs, skin and
  fat removed
2 Tbsp lite soy sauce
1 tsp brown sugar
½ cup sliced celery
¼ cup chopped onion
4 oz (½ 8-oz can) water
  chestnuts, drained and
  rinsed

8 oz mushrooms, sliced
¼ tsp garlic powder
¼ tsp powdered ginger
¼ tsp dried red pepper
  flakes
8 oz snow peas, fresh or
  frozen
1 tsp cornstarch plus
2 Tbsp cold water

METHOD

1. Place ¾ cup water and all ingredients except snow peas, cornstarch, and water in pressure cooker. Close cover securely. Place pressure regulator on vent pipe and bring to pressure on medium-high heat.
2. Cook 6 minutes with pressure regulator rocking gently.
3. Let pressure drop of its own accord (takes about 10 minutes).
4. Remove cooker lid and add snow peas, then return to a boil. Do not cover.
5. Stir in cornstarch mixed with water and simmer until thickened. Serve over rice or oriental noodles.

166

Fruit Crisp

Yield: 6 servings / Serving size: ¾ cup

INGREDIENTS

Nonstick vegetable cooking spray
3 cups sliced apples
1 16-oz can juice-packed peaches (reserve juice)
½ cup rolled oats
½ cup whole-wheat flour
¾ tsp cinnamon
¾ tsp nutmeg
¾ tsp cornstarch
2 Tbsp reduced-calorie margarine

METHOD

1. Lightly coat a 9- by 9-inch baking pan with vegetable spray.
2. Put apples and peaches in pan, along with peach juice.
3. In a separate bowl, combine oats, flour, cinnamon, nutmeg, cornstarch, and margarine. Stir half of mixture into fruit.
4. Sprinkle remainder of the dry mixture over top of the fruit and bake at 375 degrees for 30 minutes.

DINNER

3 Porcupine Meatballs
½ cup steamed carrots
1 cup celery sticks and radishes
10 small Spanish olives
1 **Baked Apple II** (page 169)

Porcupine Meatballs

Yield: 2 servings / Serving size: 3 meatballs with sauce

INGREDIENTS

8 oz ground beef
⅓ cup uncooked rice
1½ Tbsp dried minced onion
¼ tsp pepper
⅛ tsp oregano
1 cup tomato sauce

METHOD

1. Mix meat, rice, onion, and seasonings until well blended. Form into 6 equal-size meatballs.
3. Place rack in pressure cooker. Pour tomato sauce and 1½ cups water into cooker. Add meatballs.
4. Cover pressure cooker and place pressure regulator on vent pipe.
5. Heat until cooker reaches optimum pressure. Cook 12 minutes.
6. Remove from heat, and let pressure drop of its own accord.

Baked Apple II

Yield: 2 servings / Serving size: 1 apple

INGREDIENTS

2 small cooking apples
2 tsp margarine
2 tsp no-sugar-added currant or grape jelly

METHOD

1. Core apples, leaving bottom intact. Place in oven-proof baking dish with ½ inch water.
2. Put 1 tsp margarine and 1 tsp jelly in each apple.
3. Bake at 350 degrees for 30 minutes or until tender.
4. Baste with jelly-margarine mixture before serving.

DINNER

1 serving **Barbecued Chicken**
1 6-inch corn on the cob
½ cup steamed broccoli
½ cup carrot sticks
1 slice **Sally Lunn Peach Cake** (page 171)

Barbecued Chicken

Yield: 2 servings / Serving size: ½ recipe

INGREDIENTS

2 chicken thighs and 2 chicken legs
½ cup **Barbecue Sauce**

METHOD

1. Marinate raw chicken pieces in barbecue sauce at least 2 hours in the refrigerator, turning occasionally.
2. Cook on outdoor grill until chicken is no longer pink.

Barbecue Sauce

Yield: 4½ cups / Serving size: ¼ cup

INGREDIENTS

1 small onion, minced
2 8-oz cans tomato sauce
2 cups water
¼ cup wine vinegar
¼ cup Worcestershire sauce
1 tsp salt (optional)

2 tsp paprika
2 tsp chili powder
1 tsp pepper
½ tsp cinnamon
⅛ tsp ground cloves

METHOD

1. Combine all ingredients in a saucepan. Bring to a full boil.
2. Reduce heat and simmer for 20 minutes.

Sally Lunn Peach Cake

Yield: 1 loaf of 12 slices / Serving size: 1 slice

INGREDIENTS
2 cups sifted flour
3 tsp baking powder
½ tsp salt
1 egg, beaten
¾ cup skim or 1% milk
½ cup vegetable oil
¼ cup sugar
Nonstick vegetable cooking spray
Fresh or juice-packed peaches

METHOD
1. Sift flour with baking powder and salt.
2. Combine egg, milk, and oil in a large bowl. Add sugar. Stir in dry ingredients. Do not overmix.
3. Pour batter into a loaf pan that has been coated with vegetable spray.
4. Bake at 375 degrees for 30 minutes.
5. Top each slice with ⅓ cup sliced peaches.

DINNER

3 oz Fish Creole
⅔ cup cooked brown or white rice
½ cup green beans
1 peach

Fish Creole

Yield: 4 servings / Serving size: 3-oz fillet plus sauce

INGREDIENTS

4 3-oz fish fillets
Nonstick vegetable cooking spray
2 Tbsp lemon juice
2 Tbsp finely chopped onion
4 Tbsp reduced-calorie margarine
½ cup chopped green peppers
1 cup chopped canned tomatoes (reserve juice)
Pepper to taste
2 tsp flour

METHOD

1. Place fish fillets in baking pan coated with vegetable spray.
2. Mix together lemon juice, onion, and 2 Tbsp melted margarine.
3. Pour mixture over fish. Heat oven to 350 degrees and bake uncovered or until fish flakes easily with fork.
4. While fish is baking, prepare creole sauce: Sauté green pepper in remaining margarine. Add tomatoes, ½ cup juice, and pepper. Simmer until mixture is heated.

DINNER

1 serving Bok Choy Sauté
⅔ cup cooked brown rice
⅓ cup fresh pineapple chunks mixed with
½ cup fresh strawberries

61

Bok Choy Sauté

Yield: 2 servings / Serving size: ½ recipe

INGREDIENTS
1 Tbsp sesame or vegetable oil
1 clove garlic, crushed
8 oz pork tenderloin, thinly sliced
1 cup sliced shiitake or other mushrooms
1½ cups sliced bok choy, with leaves
4 oz (½ 8-oz can) water chestnuts, drained and rinsed
1 Tbsp lite soy sauce

METHOD
1. Add oil to a large skillet or wok over medium-high heat and cook garlic 1 minute.
2. Add pork, stirring constantly, and cook 3–5 minutes. Add mushrooms and cook for 1 minute, stirring constantly. Add bok choy and water chestnuts and cook, stirring constantly, 2–3 minutes.
3. Add soy sauce; toss to coat.

DINNER

2 **Black Bean Cakes** with
½ cup **Cilantro Salsa** (page 175) and
2 Tbsp low-fat sour cream
½ cup frozen yogurt

Black Bean Cakes

Yield: 2 servings / Serving size: 2 cakes

INGREDIENTS

1¼ cups cooked black beans
½ cup chopped onion
½ cup chopped fresh cilantro or parsley
2 Tbsp Korean chili-garlic paste or plain tomato paste
1 egg
2 Tbsp skim or 1% milk
Salt and pepper to taste
¼ cup bread crumbs
2 Tbsp olive oil

METHOD

1. Thoroughly mix all ingredients except bread crumbs and olive oil. Add bread crumbs to mixture and form into 4 patties.
2. Gently slide patties into an oiled, hot sauté pan. Sauté until brown and crisp on both sides.

Cilantro Salsa

Yield: 4 servings / Serving size: ½ cup

INGREDIENTS

2 tomatoes, diced
1 small cucumber, peeled and chopped
1 small red onion, diced
½ cup chopped fresh cilantro leaves
1 tsp grated lime peel
1 small green pepper, diced
1–2 dashes hot sauce
Salt and pepper to taste

METHOD

1. Blend all ingredients to desired chunkiness and chill
   overnight.

DINNER

1 serving **Jambalaya**
Tossed salad with
2 Tbsp reduced-calorie dressing
¼ cup melon cubes

Jambalaya

Yield: 4 servings / Serving size: 1½ cups

INGREDIENTS

4 oz lean ham, chopped
1 cup chopped onion
2 celery stalks, chopped
1 medium green pepper, chopped
1 28-oz can tomatoes (reserve juice)
¼ cup tomato paste
1 clove garlic, minced
1 Tbsp minced parsley
½ tsp minced thyme
2 whole cloves
1 Tbsp vegetable oil
⅔ cup uncooked brown or white rice
16 medium-large shrimp, peeled and deveined

METHOD

1. Thoroughly mix all ingredients except shrimp in a slow cooker. Cover and cook on low setting for 7–10 hours.
2. One hour before serving, turn slow cooker to high setting. Stir in uncooked shrimp. Cover and cook until shrimp are pink and tender.

2 skewers Hawaiian Kabobs
⅔ cup cooked brown or white rice
Tossed salad with
2 Tbsp reduced-calorie dressing

64

Hawaiian Kabobs

Yield: 4 servings / Serving size: 2 skewers

INGREDIENTS

1 Tbsp soy sauce
¼ cup pineapple juice
½ tsp garlic powder
1 tsp ground ginger
½ tsp dry mustard
¼ tsp pepper
2 Tbsp corn oil
14 oz chicken breast, cut into 1-inch cubes
2 cups fresh or juice-packed pineapple chunks
2 medium green peppers, cut into chunks
16 medium mushrooms
8 cherry tomatoes

METHOD

1. Combine first 7 ingredients in a small saucepan and bring to a boil. Reduce heat and simmer 5 minutes. Let cool.
2. Pour mixture into a shallow dish and add chicken, tossing gently to coat. Cover and marinate at least 1 hour in the refrigerator, stirring mixture occasionally.
3. Remove chicken from marinade, reserving marinade. Alternate chicken, pineapple, green pepper, mushrooms, and tomatoes on 8 skewers.
4. Grill over hot coals 20 minutes or until done, turning and basting frequently with marinade.

DINNER

1 serving **Apricot-Glazed Ham**
½ cup **Lightly Scalloped Potatoes**
   (page 179)
½ cup steamed green beans
1 slice reduced-calorie whole-wheat bread
   with
1 tsp reduced-calorie margarine
½ cup sugar-free lemon gelatin with
1 Tbsp whipped topping

Apricot-Glazed Ham

Yield: 4 servings / Serving size: 3 oz ham and ¼ cup glaze

INGREDIENTS
½ cup orange juice
2 Tbsp currants or raisins
1 cup juice-packed apricots, drained
¼ tsp grated or ground ginger (optional)
12-oz lean ham steak, trimmed of fat

METHOD
1. Combine orange juice, currants, apricots, and ginger in a small saucepan. Cook over medium heat until thickened, about 8–10 minutes.
2. Place ham slice on baking pan. Pour sauce over ham and bake at 350 degrees for about 20 minutes. Divide ham into 4 equal servings.

DINNER

Lightly Scalloped Potatoes

Yield: 8 servings / Serving size: ½ cup

INGREDIENTS
1 clove garlic, diced
¼ cup diced onion
2½ tsp flour
6 oz evaporated skim milk
¾ cup skim or 1% milk
½ tsp salt
¼ tsp red pepper
Nonstick vegetable cooking spray
4½ cups (2½ lb) thinly sliced red potatoes
½ cup low-fat shredded cheddar or Swiss cheese
⅓ cup Parmesan cheese

METHOD
1. In a nonstick saucepan, sauté garlic and onion until tender. Add flour and mix well. Add milk and seasonings. Cook until slightly thickened, stirring constantly, about 2 minutes.
2. Alternate layers of potato, cheese, and sauce in a 2-qt baking dish that has been coated with vegetable spray.
3. Bake at 350 degrees for 45 minutes or until bubbly and golden brown. Let stand 20 minutes before serving.

3 oz beef Western rib, grilled and basted
  with
2 Tbsp barbecue sauce
1 Pillsbury buttermilk or country-style biscuit
1 cup steamed green beans flavored with
1 slice Canadian bacon, chopped
3 oz Ore-Ida Zesties fries, baked
¾ cup **Raspberry-Orange Gelatin
  Supreme**

Raspberry-Orange Gelatin Supreme

Yield: 6 servings / Serving size: ¾ cup

INGREDIENTS

1 pkg. orange sugar-free gelatin
1 pkg. raspberry sugar-free gelatin
2 cups 100% raspberry juice
2 cups water
1 11-oz can juice-packed mandarin oranges

METHOD

1. Pour gelatin powders into a 2-qt bowl.
2. In a small pan, mix raspberry juice and water and heat
   to boiling.
3. Mix boiling juice mixture and gelatin until gelatin is
   thoroughly dissolved.
4. Chill until thickened but not completely gelled. Add
   oranges, stirring to spread throughout gelatin. Chill until
   firm.

DINNER

67

1 serving **Egg-Asparagus Casserole**
Tossed salad with
1 Tbsp fat-free dressing
1 medium whole-wheat roll
½ cup melon balls

Egg-Asparagus Casserole

Yield: 5 servings / Serving size: 1 cup

INGREDIENTS

½ cup margarine
¼ cup all-purpose whole-
   wheat flour
½ tsp salt (optional)
1½ cups skim or 1% milk
1 cup shredded low-fat mild
   cheddar cheese

⅛ tsp red pepper
2 lb fresh asparagus,
   steamed
1 cup egg substitute, cooked
½ cup cracker crumbs

METHOD

1. In a saucepan, melt ¼ cup margarine and stir in flour
   and salt; blend in enough milk to make a smooth paste.
   Stir in remainder of milk and cook over medium heat
   until sauce is thickened, stirring constantly.
2. While sauce is hot, stir in shredded cheese and red
   pepper. Stir until cheese is melted.
3. In a greased 1½-qt baking dish, layer half of the
   asparagus, eggs, and sauce. Repeat ingredients to make
   a second layer. Top with cracker crumbs mixed with ¼
   cup margarine.
4. Bake in 350-degree oven for 30 minutes or until
   mixture bubbles. Place under broiler 2 minutes to brown
   top.

DINNER

1 serving **Tofu-Vegetable Stir-Fry**
1 cup cooked brown rice
Tossed salad with
1 Tbsp dressing
1 3-inch square **Pineapple-Oatmeal Cake**
(page 183)

Tofu-Vegetable Stir-Fry

Yield: 4 servings / Serving size: 2 cups

INGREDIENTS

½ lb firm tofu, drained and cubed
2 Tbsp olive oil
4 carrots, sliced thin
1 head broccoli, chopped
1 Tbsp sunflower seeds
1 onion, sliced or chopped
1 tsp basil
4 cloves garlic, chopped
1 cup sliced mushrooms
2 Tbsp soy sauce or tamari

METHOD

1. Sauté tofu in oil. Flip cubes once or twice to brown on a few sides, about 5 minutes.
2. Add carrots and mix; then add broccoli, sunflower seeds, onions, basil, and garlic. Sauté about 3 minutes, mix, and add mushrooms.
3. Turn off heat, add soy sauce, and cover. Let steam for 1 or 2 minutes. Serve with rice or noodles.

Pineapple-Oatmeal Cake

Yield: 9 servings / Serving size: 3-inch square

INGREDIENTS
1½ cups rolled oats
3 Tbsp brown sugar substitute
3 Tbsp nonfat dry milk
4 Tbsp whole-wheat flour
2 tsp baking powder
⅛ tsp baking soda
1 tsp cinnamon
2 cups crushed juice-packed pineapple
2 eggs
2 Tbsp corn oil
Nonstick vegetable cooking spray

METHOD
1. Combine all ingredients in a large bowl. Mix well.
2. Coat a 9-inch-square pan with vegetable spray and pour in mixture.
3. Bake in 375-degree oven for 25 minutes.

DINNER

1 Bean Enchilada
1 cup steamed broccoli
⅔ cup cooked brown rice

Bean Enchilada

Yield: 8 servings / Serving size: 1 enchilada

INGREDIENTS
Sauce:
    2 tsp olive oil
    ⅓ cup finely chopped onions
    ⅓ cup finely chopped green pepper
    5 cloves garlic, minced
    1 16-oz can tomato sauce (salt-free optional)
    ½ tsp basil
    ½ tsp oregano
Filling:
    2 tsp olive oil
    1 cup chopped onions
    1 green pepper, chopped
    4 cloves garlic, minced
    1 16-oz can (about 3 cups) kidney beans, mashed
    1 cup canned or frozen corn, drained
    8 whole-wheat flour tortillas
    3 oz (about ¾ cup) shredded low-fat cheddar cheese

METHOD

1. To make sauce, sauté onions, green pepper, and garlic in oil. Cook until tender, about 5 minutes.
2. Remove from heat and add remaining sauce ingredients; set aside.
3. For filling, sauté onions, green pepper, and garlic for about 5 minutes.
4. Add mashed kidney beans, corn, and ½ cup sauce.
5. To assemble enchiladas, spread ½ cup sauce on the bottom of a 6- by 10-inch baking pan. Spread ⅓ cup bean mixture onto each tortilla. Roll up tightly and place tortillas in pan, seam side down.
6. Spoon remaining sauce over tortillas. Cover and bake in a 350-degree oven for 30 minutes.
7. Uncover, sprinkle with cheese, and bake for 5 more minutes.

DINNER

1 serving **Bean Burgers**
1 whole-wheat hamburger roll
1 cup green beans with
1 Tbsp reduced-calorie margarine
2 **Breakfast in a Cookie** (page 187)

Bean Burgers

Yield: 8 servings / Serving size: 1 burger

INGREDIENTS

1 16-oz can kidney, pinto, or black beans
2 cups cooked brown rice or millet
2 Tbsp ketchup
2 cloves garlic, minced
1 tsp dried oregano
1 tsp dried basil
¼ cup finely chopped onions
Salt and pepper to taste
Nonstick vegetable cooking spray

METHOD

1. Combine all ingredients in a large bowl and mash with a fork or potato masher.
2. Divide mixture into 8 burgers, making patties about ½ inch thick. You may need to wet your hands to keep the mixture from sticking.
3. Coat a nonstick skillet with vegetable spray. Cook burgers over medium heat until browned on both sides.

Breakfast in a Cookie

Yield: 3½–4 dozen / Serving size: 2 cookies

INGREDIENTS

⅓ cup whole-bran cereal, wheat or oat
¼ cup orange juice
¼ cup honey or ⅜ cup sugar
¼ cup no-sugar-added applesauce
1 egg or 2 egg whites
1½ tsp vanilla
1 cup whole-wheat pastry flour
1 tsp baking powder
½ tsp baking soda
⅓ cup nonfat dry milk
2 tsp grated orange rind
1 tsp cinnamon or nutmeg
1 cup regular or quick-cooking rolled oats
½ cup finely chopped nuts
1 cup raisins
Nonstick vegetable cooking spray

METHOD

1. Preheat oven to 375 degrees.
2. In a small bowl, combine bran and orange juice; set aside.
3. In a large bowl, mix honey and applesauce; add egg and mix.
4. Blend in bran–orange juice mixture and add vanilla.
5. Add remaining ingredients to wet mixture.
6. Drop by level teaspoonful onto cookie sheets coated with vegetable spray, about 2 inches apart, and bake for 10–12 minutes or until golden brown.

1 serving **Chicken Casserole**
1 small dinner roll with
1 tsp margarine
Tossed salad with
2 Tbsp reduced-calorie dressing
1 slice **Chocolate Angel Food Cake** (page
141)
1 cup raspberries, fresh or frozen,
unsweetened

Chicken Casserole

Yield: 4 servings / Serving size: 1 cup

INGREDIENTS

1 Tbsp reduced-calorie
margarine
2 Tbsp oat flour
½ tsp salt (optional)
1 cup skim or 1% milk
1 cup sliced mushrooms
2 tsp Parmesan cheese

⅔ cup cubed cooked white
meat chicken
⅔ cup chopped broccoli
florets
3 Tbsp chopped onion
2 Tbsp rolled oats

METHOD

1. Prepare white sauce by melting margarine in medium
   saucepan. Add oat flour and stir until all flour is coated
   evenly. Stir in salt. Slowly add milk, stirring constantly.
   Heat sauce to boiling, stirring frequently. Cook 1 minute
   to thicken. Use only ⅔ cup of sauce; discard remainder.
2. When sauce thickens, add mushrooms. Stir and cook 1
   minute. Remove from heat and add cheese. Mix well.
3. In medium mixing bowl, combine chicken, broccoli, and
   onion. Stir in sauce and mix well to coat all ingredients.
4. Pour into 1-qt casserole. Top with rolled oats. Bake for
   30 minutes at 350 degrees.

1 serving **Hearty Garlic Soup**
2 medium whole-wheat rolls
1 Tbsp Parmesan cheese
1 apple

Hearty Garlic Soup

Yield: 4 servings / Serving size: 1½ cups

INGREDIENTS

2 cups sliced onions
1 cup sliced green pepper
1½ Tbsp olive oil
20 garlic cloves, sliced
3 cups canned tomatoes
2 cups vegetable broth or water
3 or 4 slices dark, whole-wheat bread, cut in ¼-inch cubes
Black pepper to taste

METHOD

1. In large saucepan, sauté onions and pepper in oil until soft and golden.
2. Add garlic and tomatoes. Reduce heat, cover pan, and simmer for 30 minutes.
3. Add broth; heat to a boil.
4. Add bread cubes just before serving. Add black pepper to taste.

DINNER

1 serving **Spinach-Stuffed Chicken Breasts**
1 cup steamed new potatoes
Lettuce with
½ cup grapefruit sections,
1 Tbsp French dressing, and
1 Tbsp slivered almonds

Spinach-Stuffed Chicken Breasts

Yield: 4 servings / Serving size: ½ breast with stuffing

INGREDIENTS

½ 10-oz pkg. frozen chopped spinach, defrosted and
   drained
2 oz (¼ cup) low-fat ricotta cheese
2 oz low-fat mozzarella cheese, finely diced or shredded
¼ tsp tarragon
¼ tsp salt
⅛ tsp pepper
2 whole chicken breasts, deboned (leave skin intact)
½ tsp margarine, melted

METHOD

1. Preheat oven to 350 degrees.
2. Combine spinach, cheeses, and seasonings.
3. Lift up skin of each chicken breast and divide mixture
   evenly among them. Be careful not to tear skins.
   Smooth skin over stuffing; tuck skin edges underneath
   to form a neat package.
4. Brush chicken with melted margarine. Place in 2-qt
   baking dish.
5. Bake uncovered for 45–50 minutes.

Tortellini Primavera

Tossed green salad with
1 Tbsp fat-free dressing
½ cup skim or 1% milk

74

Tortellini Primavera

Yield: 1 serving

INGREDIENTS

½ cup fresh or frozen cheese tortellini
⅓ cup each sliced or chunked broccoli, mushrooms,
   zucchini, and asparagus
½ small clove garlic, minced
½ tsp olive oil
½ cup skim or 1% milk
1 tsp cornstarch
Pinch nutmeg
Freshly ground pepper
1 Tbsp parsley
2 Tbsp sliced green onion
2 Tbsp Parmesan cheese

METHOD

1. Boil water and cook tortellini according to package
   directions while proceeding with the vegetables.
2. Sauté vegetables and garlic in nonstick skillet with oil on
   medium-high heat for about 1 minute. Reduce heat and
   cover for 1–2 more minutes until tender-crisp.
3. Combine milk and cornstarch and add it to the
   vegetables. Stir constantly until thickened.
4. Add nutmeg and pepper to taste. Toss together with
   tortellini, parsley, and onion. Sprinkle with Parmesan
   cheese.

DINNER

1 serving **Vegetable Curry**
1 cup cooked lentils
Cafe Mocha:
   ½ cup strong coffee
   ½ cup scalded skim or 1% milk, whipped
   ½ tsp cocoa
   Artificial sweetener to taste

Mix coffee and milk in tall mug and sprinkle with sweetener and cocoa.

Vegetable Curry

Yield: 1 serving (about 2 cups)

INGREDIENTS

½ cup each sliced or
   chunked green pepper,
   red pepper, zucchini,
   broccoli, carrots, onion,
   celery, and/or mushrooms
1 tsp olive oil
¼ tsp curry powder
½ cup skim or 1% milk

1 tsp cornstarch
Freshly ground pepper to
   taste
1 medium tomato, wedged
2 Tbsp sliced green onions
1 Tbsp chopped peanuts
1 Tbsp raisins

METHOD

1. Sauté vegetables except tomato in oil until tender-crisp. Sprinkle with curry powder.
2. Combine milk and cornstarch and add to vegetables. Stir constantly until thickened.
3. Adjust seasoning by adding more curry powder and pepper. Add tomato just before serving. Serve over lentils, and sprinkle with onions, nuts, and raisins.

Snacks

Each 60-calorie snack includes
1 Starch serving OR
1 Fruit serving OR
2 Vegetable servings

Each 125-calorie snack includes
1 Starch serving and
1 Fat serving OR
1 Meat Substitute serving and
1 Fruit serving

Each 170-calorie snack includes
1 Starch serving and
1 Skim Milk serving OR
2 Starch servings OR
1 Starch serving and
1 Meat serving

60-Calorie Snacks

½ cup strawberries
4 animal crackers

1 Dole Fruit and Juice Bar

1 cup carrot sticks with
1 Tbsp ranch dressing

16 fat-free tortilla chips with
Salsa

Grapefruit Cooler:
   8 oz sugar-free ginger ale and
   $\frac{1}{2}$ cup grapefruit juice

Macedonia Fruit Cup

Yield: 10 servings / Serving size: ½ cup

INGREDIENTS

¾ cup orange juice
4 tsp lemon juice
15 seedless grapes
12 cherries, pitted
1 apple, peeled and thinly sliced
1 pear, peeled and thinly sliced
1 banana, peeled and thinly sliced
1 plum, thinly sliced
1 peach, thinly sliced
⅛ honeydew melon, cubed
¾ cup strawberries, halved
Artificial sweetener to taste

METHOD

1. Pour orange and lemon juice into a large serving bowl. Add seedless grapes and cherries.
2. Add each other fruit to the bowl immediately after cutting it to prevent discoloration.
3. Serve chilled.

½ cup **Fruit Punch**

Fruit Punch

Yield: 12 servings / Serving size: ½ cup

INGREDIENTS

2 cups unsweetened pineapple juice, chilled
2 cups cranberry juice cocktail, chilled
¾ cup orange juice, chilled
¾ cup club soda, chilled
Ice cubes
Lime slices

METHOD

1. Combine the chilled ingredients in a punch bowl just before serving.

Frosty Grapes

Yield: 4 servings / Serving size: about 15 grapes

INGREDIENTS

1 lb seedless grapes
1 3-oz pkg. sugar-free lime gelatin

METHOD

1. Divide grapes into small bunches. Rinse and drain.
2. Put gelatin powder in a container with a lid that can be frozen. Add grapes and shake to coat. Shake off excess powder from grape bunches.
3. Put lid on container and freeze. Serve frozen.

½ frozen banana on a stick dipped in
2 Tbsp **Chocolate-Flavored Syrup**

Chocolate-Flavored Syrup

Yield: 15 servings / Serving size: 2 Tbsp

INGREDIENTS

½ cup dry cocoa, firmly packed
1½ cups cold water
¼ tsp salt
Artificial sweetener to substitute for ½ cup sugar
2½ tsp vanilla

METHOD

1. Mix cocoa, water, and salt in a heavy saucepan until
   smooth. Bring to a boil and simmer gently, stirring
   constantly, for 3 minutes.
2. Remove from heat and let cool 10 minutes.
3. Add artificial sweetener and vanilla and mix well.
4. Store refrigerated in a jar. Stir well in jar before
   measuring to use.

Strawberry Whip

Yield: 4 servings / Serving size: ¾ cup

INGREDIENTS

3-oz box sugar-free gelatin
8 oz nonfat plain yogurt
1 cup sliced strawberries

METHOD

1. Prepare gelatin according to instructions on package.
2. Beat hardened gelatin with rotary beater until frothy. Add yogurt and beat gently until mixed.
3. Stir strawberries into gelatin-yogurt mixture.
4. Freeze 10 minutes, then serve.

125-Calorie Snacks

1 cup tomato soup
4 crackers

1 cup popcorn
¼ oz pretzels
¼ cup Cheerios cereal
20 small peanuts

Mix together for party or trail mix.

½ slice angel food cake topped with
½ cup sliced strawberries and
1 Tbsp whipped topping

1 slice French bread, broiled with
1 tsp reduced-calorie margarine
1 Tbsp Parmesan cheese and
Basil

4 RyKrisp crackers, divided into 12 sections,
   with
Cheese Spread:
   1½ Tbsp low-fat cream cheese
   1 tsp dried onion flakes, and topped with
Cucumber, red pepper, and green onion
   slices

No-Fat Steak Fries

Slice a medium-large left-over baked potato with skin into wedges and place on nonstick cookie sheet. Spray with butter-flavored nonstick vegetable cooking spray and broil until golden.

$\frac{1}{3}$ cup low-fat cottage cheese
$\frac{1}{4}$ cup canned, drained pineapple chunks,
  packed in juice or water
1 Tbsp raisins

$\frac{1}{2}$ cup water-packed canned fruit with
1 cup nonfat artificially sweetened yogurt

1 oz string cheese
1 small apple

⅓ cup **Black Bean Dip** with
Vegetable chips (sliced raw carrots,
    cauliflower, broccoli, and celery)

Black Bean Dip

Yield: 2 cups / Serving size: ⅓ cup

INGREDIENTS

1 15-oz can black beans, drained
1 small onion, chopped
1 small green pepper, chopped
1 clove garlic, chopped
1½ Tbsp red wine vinegar
1½ Tbsp olive oil
½ tsp sugar
Salt, pepper, hot sauce to taste

METHOD

1. Combine all ingredients in a food processor.
2. Process, pushing off and on until beans are coarsely mashed.
3. Season to taste.

170-Calorie Snacks

½ Meat Sandwich:
   1 slice bread
   1 oz turkey or ham
   1 tsp margarine or mayonnaise

2 slices French bread toast with
2 tsp no-sugar-added fruit spread

1 Mini Pizza:
   ½ English muffin
   2 tsp pizza sauce
   1 oz part-skim mozzarella cheese

½ bagel with
1 Tbsp peanut butter

SNACKS

2 Baked Potato Skins

Split baked potatoes in half and scoop out all but ¹/₈–¹/₄ inch of potato flesh; sprinkle with 1 oz grated part-skim mozzarella cheese and paprika, then bake in 450-degree oven or broil until cheese melts and bubbles.

24 Oyster Hors D'Oeuvres

Mix 24 oyster crackers with 1 Tbsp melted margarine. Sprinkle with a powdered reduced-calorie ranch salad dressing. Broil until browned.

2 Graham Pudding Sandwiches (page 29)

Vanilla Milkshake

Yield: 1 serving / Serving size: 1½ cups

INGREDIENTS
½ cup low-fat frozen yogurt
1 cup skim or 1% milk
Vanilla extract to taste

METHOD
1. Blend all ingredients together in blender.

1 Peachy Whole-Grain Cookie
8 oz skim or 1% milk

Peachy Whole-Grain Cookie

Yield: 30 cookies / Serving size: 1 cookie

INGREDIENTS
1 egg white
½ tsp almond extract
⅓ cup margarine
⅜ cup sugar
⅜ cup packed brown sugar
¾ cup whole-wheat flour
½ tsp salt
1 tsp baking powder
1¼ cups quick-cooking or regular rolled oats
¾ cup diced peaches
¼ cup chopped dates

METHOD
1. Beat egg white with extract, margarine, and sugars in mixing bowl.
2. Combine flour, salt, and baking powder. Add to egg mixture and mix well with electric mixer.
3. Stir in oats, peaches, and dates.
4. Drop by rounded (not heaping) tablespoonful onto nonstick cookie sheet.
5. Bake at 350 degrees for 15 minutes or until golden.

SNACKS

208

10 Tortilla Chips
½ cup **Oklahoma Bean Salad**

Cut fresh or frozen corn tortillas into 6 wedges and place on a baking sheet. Bake for 5 minutes in a preheated 500-degree oven. Cool and store in airtight container.

Oklahoma Bean Salad

Yield: 5 cups / Serving size: ½ cup

INGREDIENTS
1 15-oz can black-eyed peas, rinsed and drained
2 15-oz cans garbanzo beans, rinsed and drained
2 medium tomatoes, chopped
4 green onions or ½ small onion, finely chopped
2 cloves garlic, minced
2 jalapeno peppers, finely chopped (optional)
½ cup fat-free Italian dressing
1 tsp dried oregano
1 tsp dried basil

METHOD
1. Mix all ingredients and refrigerate. Let stand for at least 2 hours before serving to let flavors blend.

SNACKS

Index

This index groups the recipes found in *Magic Menus* by main ingredient or type of food, for instance, chicken or dessert. There is also a heading called Potpourri, where you will find unique recipes, such as breakfast foods, dips, and sandwiches.

Other Books by The American Diabetes Association

Cookbooks

Diabetic Meals In 30 Minutes—Or Less!
Put an end to bland, time-consuming meals with more than 140 fast, flavorful recipes. Complete nutrition information accompanies every recipe, and a number of "quick tips" will have you out of the kitchen and into the dining room even faster! Here's a quick sample: Salsa Salad, Oven-Baked Parmesan Zucchini, Roasted Red Pepper Soup, and Layered Vanilla Parfait. #CCBDM
Nonmember: $11.95; ADA Member: $9.55

Diabetes Meal Planning Made Easy
Learn quick and easy ways to eat more starches, fruits, vegetables, and milk; make realistic changes in your eating habits to reach your diabetic goals; and understand how to use the Nutrition Facts on food labels. You'll also master the intricacies of each food group in the new Diabetes Food Pyramid and learn how much of what foods to eat to fit your personal nutrition needs. #CCBMP
Nonmember: $14.95; ADA Member: $11.95

Flavorful Seasons Cookbook
Now you can warm up your winter with recipes for Christmas, welcome spring with an Easter recipe, and cool off those hot summer days with more recipes for the Fourth of July. More than 400 unforgettable choices that combine great taste with all the good-for-you benefits of a well-balanced meal. Choose from Cornish Game Hens, Orange Sea Bass, Ginger Bread Pudding, many others. #CCBFS
Nonmember: $16.95; ADA Member: $13.55

The Healthy HomeStyle Cookbook
Here's home cooking at its best—and healthiest. Choose from more than 150 good-for-you recipes you'd love to see on the dinner table. Each recipe is low in fat, cholesterol, sugar, and calories, and each includes American Diabetes Association–approved exchanges. Also includes energy- and time-saving tips, how-tos for microwaving and freezing, and good ideas for cutting fat and calories in your meals. Special lay-flat binding allows hands-free reference while you cook. Some homestyle favorites: Sweet and Sour Meatballs, Meatless Lasagna, Rhubarb-Banana Bake, or "Guiltless" Cheesecake. #CCBHHS
Nonmember: $12.50; ADA Member: $9.95

Sweet Kids: How to Balance Diabetes Control & Good Nutrition With Family Peace
Based on a survey of 50 pediatric diabetes clinicians and parents of children with diabetes, this new guide addresses behavioral and developmental issues surrounding nutrition management in the families of children with diabetes. Each chapter begins with a story of a child with diabetes to help introduce you to each of the book's topics. *Sweet Kids* is warm, practical, and easy to understand. #CSMSK
Nonmember: $14.95; ADA Member: $11.95

Month of Meals
When celebrations begin, go ahead—dig in! The original "automatic menu planner" includes a Special Occasion section that offers tips for brunches, holidays, parties, and restaurants to give you a delicious dining options anytime, anywhere. Menu choices include Chicken Cacciatore, Oven Fried Fish, Sloppy Joes, Crab Cakes, and many others. #CMPMOM
Nonmember: $12.50; ADA Member: $9.95

Month of Meals 2

Automatic menu planning goes ethnic! A healthy diet doesn't have to keep you from your favorite restaurants. Tips and meal suggestions for Mexican, Italian, and Chinese restaurants are featured. Quick-to-fix and ethnic recipes are also included. Menu choices include Beef Burritos, Chop Suey, Veal Piccata, Stuffed Peppers, and many others. #CMPMOM2
Nonmember: $12.50; ADA Member: $9.95

Month of Meals 3

Enjoy fast food without guilt! Make sensible but delicious choices at McDonald's, Wendy's, Taco Bell, Kentucky Fried Chicken, and other fast food restaurants. Special sections offer valuable tips such as reading ingredient labels, preparing meals for picnics, and meal planning when you're ill. Menu choices include Fajita in a Pita, Seafood Stir Fry, Stouffer's Macaroni and Cheese, and many others. #CMPMOM3
Nonmember: $12.50; ADA Member: $9.95

Month of Meals 4

Meat and potatoes menu planning! Beef up your meal planning with old-time family favorites like Meatloaf and Pot Roast, Crispy Fried Chicken, Beef Stroganoff, Kielbasa and Sauerkraut, Sausage and Cornbread Pie, and many others. Hints for turning family-size meals into delicious left-overs will keep generous portions from going to waste. Meal plans for one or two people are also featured. Spiral-bound. #CMPMOM4
Nonmember: $12.50; ADA Member: $9.95

Month of Meals 5

Meatless meals picked fresh from the garden. Choose from a garden of fresh vegetarian selections like Eggplant Italian, Stuffed Zucchini, Cucumbers with Dill Dressing, Vegetable Lasagna, and many others. Plus, you'll reap all the health benefits of a vegetarian diet, including less obesity, less coronary artery disease, less colon and lung cancer, less osteoporosis, and more. #CMPMOM5
Nonmember: $12.50; ADA Member: $9.95

Self-Care

American Diabetes Association Complete Guide to Diabetes

Every area of self-care is covered in this ultimate diabetes reference for your home. With it, you can solve problems with hundreds of hints, tips, and tricks that are proven to work. Already a best-seller, this remarkable book is easy to read and easy to use, compiled from 25 of the most respected diabetes and health experts in America. It covers insulin use. Blood sugar control. Sex and pregnancy. Eating and weight control. Insurance. Mastering diabetes supplies. Every aspect of your daily and professional life. You'll turn to this all-in-one guide again and again! #CSMCGD
Nonmember: $29.95; ADA Member: $23.95

101 Tips for Staying Healthy with Diabetes

A "must-have" guidebook! Get the inside track on the latest tips, techniques, and strategies for preventing and treating diabetes complications. You'll find simple, practical suggestions for avoiding complications through close blood-sugar control, plus easy-to-follow treatment strategies for slowing and even halting the progression of existing complications. You'll also learn how to treat and prevent skin infections, which cold and flu medicines to avoid, and how to eat the foods you like while reducing your calorie intake. #CSMFSH
Nonmember: $12.50; ADA Member: $9.95

101 Tips for Improving Your Blood Sugar
Keeping your blood sugar near normal is extremely important—it not only makes you feel better, but it also reduces the risk of developing diabetes-related complications such as nerve, eye, and kidney disease. No matter where you are, no matter what you're doing, *101 Tips* gives you the answers. One blood-sugar related question appears on each page. The answers, or tips, appear below each question. Tips cover diet, exercise, travel, weight loss, insulin injection and rotation, illness, sex, and much more. Now it's a snap to learn all about blood sugar, what affects it, and everything you can do to control it. #CSMTBBGC
Nonmember: $12.50; ADA Member: $9.95

How to Get Great Diabetes Care
This important new book explains the American Diabetes Association Standards of Care and informs you—step by step—of the importance of seeking medical attention that meets these standards. You'll learn all about special concerns and treatment options for gestational diabetes, diabetic eye disease and retinopathy, diabetic nephropathy, hypertension, and foot care. Included are discussions on the different types of diabetes, the goals of treatment, how to choose and effectively talk to your doctor, and much more. #CSMHGGDC
Nonmember: $11.95; ADA Member: $9.55

How to Order

1. **To order by phone:** just call us at **1 800 ADA-ORDER** and have your credit card ready. VISA, MasterCard, and American Express are accepted. Please mention code CKA96MM when ordering.

2. **To order by mail:** on a separate sheet of paper, write down the books you're ordering and calculate the total using the shipping & handling chart below. (NOTE: Virginia residents add 4.5% sales tax; Georgia residents add 6.0% sales tax.) Then include your check, written to the American Diabetes Association, with your order and mail to:

American Diabetes Association
Order Fulfillment Department
P.O. Box 930850
Atlanta, GA 31193-0850

Shipping & Handling Chart
up to $30.00 .... add $3.00
$30.01–50.00 .... add $4.00
over $50.00 .... add 8%

Allow 2–3 weeks for shipment. Add $3.00 to shipping & handling for each extra shipping address. Add $15 for each overseas shipment. Prices subject to change without notice.